Acknowledgements
There are many people I'd like to thank for their help with this, my first book. Firstly I would like
to thank Culpitt for their help, especially Jane in the samples room to whom no request was a problem.
To Corinne, who has nursed me through the minefield of editing. To Ed for his professionalism
and fantastic photography and to the tank commander for his laughter.

My everlasting thanks to my best friend and business partner, Joyce Lisle. This is another fine mess
you've got me into, pal! Last but by no means least, thanks to my family. All my love and thanks to Alan,
my husband, and to my three wonderful daughters, Victoria, Philippa and Jessica, and to Carl for
putting up with my tempers and tantrums during the writing of this book.

**I would like to dedicate this book to Alice and Bill Wilkinson,
the greatest parents anyone could ever have.**

First published in 2005 by New Holland Publishers (UK) Ltd
London • Cape Town • Sydney • Auckland

Garfield House
86–88 Edgware Road
London W2 2EA
United Kingdom
www.newhollandpublishers.com

80 McKenzie Street
Cape Town 8001
South Africa

Level 1, Unit 4
14 Aquatic Drive
Frenchs Forest
NSW 2086
Australia

218 Lake Road
Northcote
Auckland
New Zealand

ISBN 1 84537 045 7

Senior Editor: Corinne Masciocchi
Design: AG&G Books
Production: Hazel Kirkman
Photography: Edward Allwright
Editorial Direction: Rosemary Wilkinson

1 3 5 7 9 10 8 6 4 2

Reproduction by Pica Digital PTE Ltd, Singapore
Printed and bound by Times Offset (M) Sdn. Bhd., Malaysia

Contents

Introduction

Since I first started cake decorating, my style has always tended towards the modern and flamboyant, so when I was asked to write a book called *Fantastic Party Cakes*, my imagination took flight. The use of bold colours, feathers, pearls and dragees give the designs in this book a contemporary feel for a modern-day setting.

I have tried to include as many different mediums and techniques for all levels of ability, ranging from complete beginners to the more advanced cake decorators. Covering cakes, colouring pastes, modelling, piping and run-outs are just some of the techniques featured. By following the simple step-by-step instructions, beginners will be able to make stunning cakes with great results. For the more advanced cake decorators, I hope that my designs will act as a springboard for your imagination and allow you to expand my ideas into designs that suit your every need.

This book features a cake for everyone and for every occasion, whether you are celebrating a new arrival in the family, a wedding, a birthday or just want to let somebody know you love them!

For best results, read through the tools and equipment and the techniques sections at the front of the book. Don't feel that you have to own every tool featured in the book. Start off with the basics and you can built up your collection gradually. The more experienced you become, the more you'll end up adding to your tool box!

Read through the instructions before embarking on a project, then get started, have a go and delight in your creations! Enjoy the book and enjoy the cakes.

Allison

Tools and equipment

Featured here are some of the basic tools and equipment used throughout the book that you should have in your tool box.

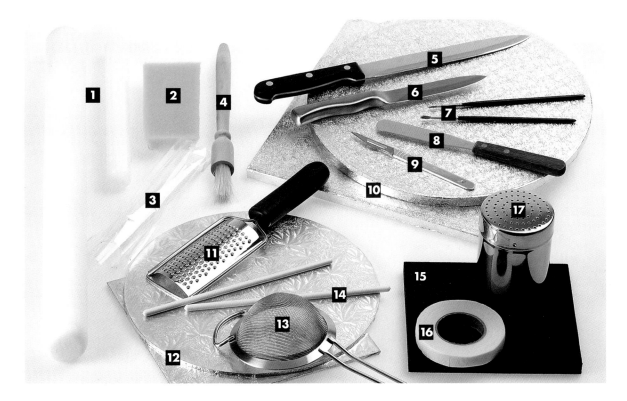

BASIC EQUIPMENT

1 Non-stick rolling pins ideal for rolling out sugar paste. Wooden rolling pins should not be used for this purpose as the paste tends to stick to the surface.

2 Sponge for drying this type of sponge is used for drying cut-out sugar paste shapes.

3 Cellophane wrap secured over a board, it is used to run out royal iced off-pieces.

4 Pastry brush make sure you invest in a good quality brush as cheaper brushes tend to lose hairs.

5 Large knife used to level the tops of cakes. Make sure the blade is sharp and always cut away from you.

6 Small sharp knife used to trim off excess sugar paste or marzipan. Regularly wipe the blade clean to avoid a sugar built up.

7 Paintbrushes the fine hairs should be undamaged so that you can paint with accuracy.

8 Palette knife used to remove delicate run-outs from cellophane wrap.

9 Craft knife used for precision cutting. Remember to cut away from you as the blade is very sharp.

10 Drum boards board on which the final cake sits. These are slightly thicker and stronger than hard boards.

11 Grater use this simple tool to make markings on marzipan shapes.

12 Spare boards used to rest cakes on when covering with marzipan or sugar paste.

13 Sieve push softened sugar paste through the sieve to make realistic grass and bushes.

14 Food-grade dowels used to support cakes that are being stacked.

15 Softening sponge slightly denser than regular sponge, it is ideal as a base on which to soften the edges of flower petals and leaves.

16 Low tack tape used to secure templates or cellophane wrap to hard boards.

17 Sugar shaker shake small amounts of icing (confectioner's) sugar onto your work surface to avoid paste from sticking to it.

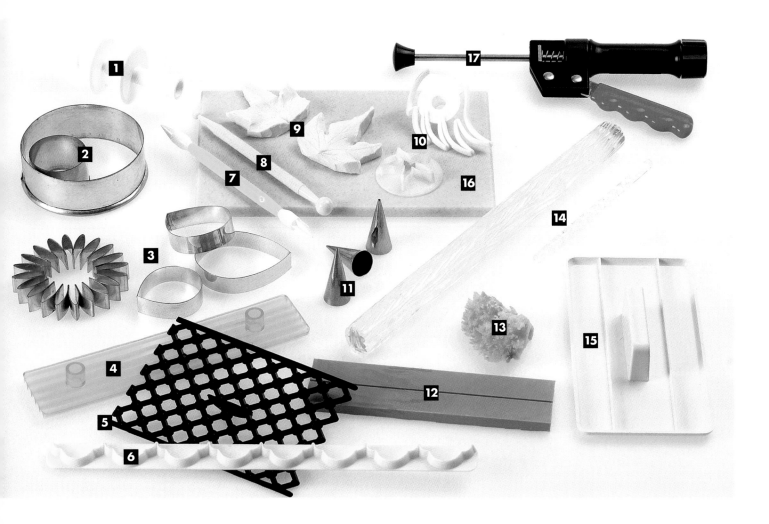

UTENSILS

1 **Ribbon cutter** used to cut strips of sugar paste or marzipan. Simply roll the tool over the rolled-out paste to achieve perfect strips.

2 **Round cutters** used to cut out circles or semi-circles. You can use scone cutters too.

3 **Metal cutters** these come in all shapes and sizes and can be bought from most sugarcraft shops.

4 **Strip cutter** ideal for cutting thin strips of sugar paste if you find it hard to cut freehand.

5 **Decorative embosser** these come in various styles and designs and can be bought from most sugarcraft shops.

6 **Patterned strip cutter** used to create a pretty edge to strips of sugar paste.

7 **Ridge cone tool** used for adding extra detail to models and flowers.

8 **Ball tool** a versatile tool used to soften the edges of leaves and petals and for making round indentations in modelling.

9 **Leaf veiners** used to mark realistic veins on leaves.

10 **Plastic cutters** used to stamp out shapes of all sizes and designs.

11 **Piping nozzles** used for piping shell borders around the base of cakes and for run-outs.

12 **Bead cutter** available in various sizes, you can make sugar paste beads to accessorize cakes.

13 **Natural sponge** use it dipped in diluted food colouring to create gentle sponge effects.

14 **Fabric texture roller** gives a fabric effect when rolled over sugar paste. These come in various designs to create a number of decorative effects.

15 **Cake smoother** used to give marzipan and sugar paste a smooth, polished finish.

16 **Non-stick board** this small board is ideal for rolling and shaping small pieces of sugar paste.

17 **Sugarcraft gun** ideal for making many shapes, including ropes to decorate the base of cakes. For best results, soften the sugar paste with a few drops of water first.

DECORATIONS AND TRIMS

1&2 Dusting colours used to enhance the colour of flowers or leaves. Apply with a soft dusting brush then steam lightly to seal the colour.

3 Food colouring use to colour sugar paste, royal icing and marzipan. Add a few drops at a time until you achieve the right colour.

4 Gold scintillo this piping gel is ideal to give a jewelled finish to almost anything.

5 Gold and silver dragees these pretty balls are edible and come in other metallic colours. Use tweezers if you find them hard to handle with your fingers.

6 Food-grade picks insert wires into them as opposed to directly into the cake.

7 Gold and silver wires these come in many different colours and are ideal to decorate all kinds of cakes.

8 Isopropyl alcohol used to blend dusting colours. The alcohol evaporates more quickly than water and the painted item dries more evenly.

9 Ribbon used to decorate the edge of drum boards.

HANDY HINTS AND TIPS

◆ Remove unwanted air bubbles in sugar paste by popping them with a sterilized pin.

◆ When modelling with marzipan, roll it between the palms of your hands to slightly heat the paste. This will get rid of any cracks, will make it more manageable and will bring out the shine in the marzipan.

◆ If flower paste is hard to work, it can be softened with a little fresh egg white to make it more pliable. Add the egg white a little at a time.

◆ If sugar paste is hard to work, it can be softened by placing it in the microwave on full heat for a few seconds – but be careful not to over heat it.

Techniques

All the fruit cakes featured in this book are covered in both marzipan and sugar paste. The sponge cakes are covered in sugar paste only.

LEVELLING THE CAKE

An easy way to level a cake is to place it back into the tin it was baked in and use the top of the tin as a guide for your knife. Make sure the blade is long enough and run it level over the top of the tin. If the cake has not risen above the tin, place a drum board beneath the cake in the bottom of the tin to raise it and cut as above. With a little experience, you will be able to level the cake free-hand.

BRUSHING THE CAKE WITH APRICOT GLAZE

See page 12 for the apricot glaze recipe. Turn the levelled cake upside down onto a spare board larger than the cake. If there is a gap between what is now the bottom of the cake and the board, fill it with a sausage of marzipan. Smooth the sides level by filling in any visible holes with small pieces of marzipan. Using a pastry brush, brush the apricot glaze all over the top and sides of the cake.

COVERING THE CAKE WITH MARZIPAN

To make the marzipan pliable, knead it on a clean surface lightly dusted with icing (confectioner's) sugar. For ease of use, you can put the icing sugar in a sugar shaker. Using a large non-stick rolling pin, roll it out evenly so that it is large enough to cover the top and sides of the cake. The use of spacers can be helpful for this. The size of the rolled out marzipan can also be measured using a piece of string. Take the string up one side of the cake, across the top and down the other side. This will give you a rough guide to the size needed. Roll out the marzipan just a little larger than this measurement.

Carefully lift the marzipan onto the cake and gently smooth the top with your hands to remove any air bubbles. Gently ease the paste onto the sides and smooth down with your hands. Run a cake smoother over the top and sides to give a smooth, polished look and then trim off the excess with a small sharp knife.

Smoothing the marzipan with the cake smoother

COVERING THE CAKE WITH SUGAR PASTE

Colour the sugar paste if required with food colouring (see page 13). Using a large non-stick rolling pin, roll out the sugar paste evenly on a clean surface lightly dusted with icing (confectioner's) sugar so that it is large enough to cover the top and sides of the cake. Avoid using too much icing sugar as this will dry out the paste and make it crack. When rolling out the sugar paste, spacers can be used to help maintain an even thickness.

Using a pastry brush, brush the marzipan with cooled boiled water. Place the sugar paste onto the cake and gently smooth the top with your hands to remove any air bubbles and to stick the paste to the cake. Ease the paste onto the sides and smooth with your hands. Take care when doing this as the paste can tear easily. If it tears, gently rock the cake smoother over the tear until it is smooth. Trim off the excess with a small sharp knife. Run a cake smoother over the top and sides of the cake to polish the surface.

COVERING THE DRUM BOARD

The amount of sugar paste needed to cover the board is included in the quantity given for the cake. Lightly dampen the board with water to help the paste stick. Roll out the sugar paste so that it is large enough to cover the surface of the board and position it onto the board. Work with a cake smoother to give a polished surface and trim off the excess with a small sharp knife. At this point the board can be given a 'fabric effect' using one of the patterned rolling pins, if desired. Set aside to dry for a couple of hours then place the covered cake over the drum board. Once the cake has been decorated, finish off the edge of the board with ribbon using double-sided sticky tape to secure it in place.

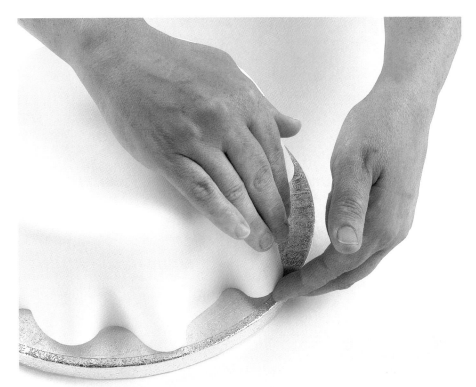

Covering the marzipan with sugar paste

Trimming off the excess sugar paste

DOWELLING THE CAKES

When stacking cakes you will need to strengthen the cakes underneath to support the weight. Place each cake that is being stacked onto a hard board the same size as the cake. Cover the cake and board with marzipan and sugar paste and leave to skim over. Insert three food-grade dowels into the bottom cake and mark them to that length. Pull them out and, using a serrated knife, score around the marks and snap the dowels. Reinsert the dowels into the cake and stack the cake layers while they are still a little soft as this gives them a chance to settle into each other. Use a little royal icing to sandwich the surface of the cake below to the board of the cake above.

Fill any gaps between the stacked cakes with softened sugar paste of the same colour. Stacked cakes can be heavy, so be careful when moving the cakes around as the sugar paste can crack. Placing the bottom tier on two boards stuck together with double-sided tape can alleviate this problem and also gives a nice finish to a cake.

Measuring the dowels

Inserting the dowels

MAKING A PIPING BAG

Cut a piece of greaseproof paper into a triangle, keeping the longest side closest to you. Holding on to one point, fold it over the palm of your hand then fold over again. You should now have a cone shape. Tuck the top edges into the inside of the bag to secure it in place. Finally, cut the tip off the bag and drop in the nozzle.

Folding the paper into a cone shape

Tucking in the tips to secure the bag

Recipes

The baking times for the cakes are approximate as every oven is slightly different. Square cakes take a little longer to bake than round ones. See baking times below.

FRUIT CAKE RECIPES

Round cake tins of the same size as square cake tins take less mixture. Follow the quantities below to achieve perfect results. Quantities outside brackets are for round cakes, and quantities in square brackets are for square cakes. If you have a fan-assisted oven you may need to turn the temperature down a little.

Round cake [Square cake]	15-cm (6-in) 15-cm (6-in)	21-cm (8-in) 21-cm (8-in)	25-cm (10-in) 25-cm (10-in)	28-cm (11-in) –	30-cm (12-in) –
Butter	75g/2½oz/⅓c [150g/5½oz/¾c]	175g/6oz/¾c [275g/9½oz/1¼c]	350g/12½oz/1½c [500g/1lb2oz/2¼c]	500g/1lb2oz/2¼c	600g/1lb5oz/2½c
Brown sugar	75g/2½oz/½c [150g/5½oz/1c]	175g/6oz/¾c [275g/9½oz/1½c]	350g/12½oz/2¼c [500g/1lb2oz/3¼c]	500g/1lb2oz/2¼c	600g/1lb5oz/2½c
Eggs (medium)	1 [2]	3 [5]	6 [9]	9	11
Ground almonds (optional)	25g/1oz/⅓c [50g/2oz/½c]	50g/2oz/½c [75g/2½oz/¾c]	100g/3½oz/¾c [150g/5½oz/1c]	150g/5½oz/1c	200g/7oz/1½c
Plain (all-purpose) flour	100g/3½oz/¾c [175g/6oz/1½c]	200g/7oz/1¾c [350g/12½oz/3c]	400g/14oz/3½c [600g/1lb5oz/5¼c]	600g/1lb5oz/5¼c	700g/1lb9oz/6¼c
Ground cinnamon	½ tsp [½ tsp]	¾ tsp [1 tsp]	1½ tsps [2 tsps]	2 tsps	2½ tsps
Mixed spice	¼ tsp [¼ tsp]	½ tsp [¾ tsp]	1 tsp [1¼ tsp]	1¼ tsps	1½ tsps
Glacé cherries, halved	40g/1½oz/½c [65g/2¼oz/¾c]	75g/2½oz/¾c [100 g/3½ oz/1 c]	150g/5½oz/1c [225g/8oz/1½c]	225g/8oz/1½c	300g/10½oz/2c
Currants	150g/5½oz/¾c [225g/8oz/1⅓c]	350g/12½oz/2c [450g/1lb/3c]	625g/1lb6oz/4c [775g/1lb11oz/4¾c]	775g/1lb11oz/5¼c	1.2kg/2lb10oz/8c
Mixed peel	25g/1oz/¼c [50g/2oz/⅓c]	50g/2oz/⅓c [75g/2½oz/½c]	100g/3½oz/½c [150g/5½oz/1c]	150g/5½oz/¾c	200g/7oz/1¼c
Raisins	50g/2oz/⅓c [90g/3oz/½c]	125g/4½oz/¾c [200 g/7 oz/1¼ c]	225g/8oz/1⅓c [375g/13oz/2¼c]	375g/13oz/2¼c	400g/14oz/2⅓c
Sultanas (white raisins)	50g/2 oz/⅓c [90g/3oz/½c]	125g/4½oz/¾ c [200g/7oz/1¼c]	225g/8oz/1⅓c [375g/13oz/2¼c]	375g/13oz/2¼c	400g/14oz/2⅓c
Baking time	**2 [2½] hrs**	**2¾ [3¼] hrs**	**3¾ [4¼–4½] hrs**	**4¼–4½ hrs**	**5¼–5½ hrs**

METHOD

Place the butter in a large mixing bowl and beat until soft. Beat in the sugar until light then gradually add a small portion of egg at a time until fully incorporated. Stir in the almonds, if using, then lightly fold in the flour, cinnamon and mixed spice until the mixture is fully incorporated. Finally, add all the fruit and stir thoroughly but do not beat. Spoon the mixture into a lightly buttered and lined cake tin. Place in the centre of a preheated oven at 150° C (300° F), gas mark 2.

SPONGE CAKE RECIPES

Sponge cakes can be nicer in the summer or for a children's birthday cake. However, the more heavily-decorated cakes take too much decoration time to allow the use of sponge which does not stay fresh for as long as a fruit cake.

21-cm (8-in) round or heart-shaped cake
- 150 g/5½ oz/¾ c butter
- 150 g/5½ oz/¾ c caster (superfine) sugar
- 3 large eggs
- 150 g/5½ oz/1¼ c self-raising flour
- 75 g/2½ oz/½ c plain (all-purpose) flour
- Rind of 1 lemon
- 1 tbsp lemon juice

Bake for 1 hour

25-cm (10-in) petal-shaped cake
- 250 g/9 oz/1 c butter
- 250 g/9 oz/1¼ c caster (superfine) sugar
- 5 large eggs
- 250 g/9 oz/2¼ c self-raising flour
- 125 g/4½ oz/1 c plain (all-purpose) flour
- Rind of 2 lemons
- 2 tbsps lemon juice

Bake for 1¼ hours

METHOD

In a large mixing bowl, cream the butter and sugar together until smooth. Beat in the eggs, one at a time, with a tablespoonful of flour. Sift in the remaining flours together and fold into the mixture along with the lemon rind and juice. Spoon into a lightly buttered and lined cake tin and smooth the surface with a spatula. Place in the centre of a preheated oven at 160° C (325° F), gas mark 3.

TIP: To check if a cake is baked, lightly press its centre. If it springs back and is golden brown, it is cooked. Take the cake out of the oven and let it rest for five minutes before turning it out onto a wire rack. Peel away the lining paper.

APRICOT GLAZE

Heat 2 heaped tablespoons of apricot jam with one tablespoon of water per cake to be glazed in a pan and bring to the boil. Sieve to remove any fruit pieces then return to the boil for a couple of minutes. Set aside to cool before using.

ROYAL ICING

Make sure that all the utensils are washed and dried thoroughly to ensure that they are clean and free from grease. The quantities here make 500 g (1 lb 2 oz) of royal icing.

- 2–3 large egg whites
- 450 g/1 lb/3¼ c icing (confectioner's) sugar, sifted

Place the egg whites into a mixing bowl and remove any strings. Beat them with a folk until frothy. Do not use a whisk as this will incorporate too much air into the whites. Gradually add the sifted icing sugar to the egg white mixture, beating gently all the time until it is fully incorporated into the mixture. Continue to beat with a fork until the royal icing is smooth and is of a soft peak consistency.

TIP: Always keep royal icing covered as it will skim over quickly. If it has been standing a while, you will need to beat it again before using.

If you prefer to use albumen powder instead of egg whites the recipe would be as follows:

- 3 tsps albumen powder mixed with 90 ml/3 fl oz cold water
- 450 g/1 lb/3¼ c icing (confectioner's) sugar, sifted

In a mixing bowl, mix the albumen powder and water together until frothy. Gradually add the sifted icing sugar to the albumen mixture, beating gently all the time with a wooden spoon until it is fully incorporated into the mixture. Continue to beat until the royal icing is smooth and is of a soft peak consistency.

Colouring royal icing
You can colour royal icing with food colouring. Add a few drops at a time until the right colour mix is achieved.

BUTTERCREAM

- 125 g/4½ oz/½ c softened butter
- 375 g/13 oz/2½ c icing (confectioner's) sugar, sifted
- 1 tbsp milk

Place the butter into a mixing bowl. Gradually add the sifted icing sugar beating with a wooden spoon until soft. At the same time add the milk. Continue to beat until smooth and creamy. Refrigerated, buttercream keeps for one week stored in an airtight container.

SUGAR GLUE

Sugar glue can be made by melting a walnut-size piece of sugar paste mixed with 2 tablespoons water.

PASTILLAGE

Commercial pastillage is available from sugarcraft shops but to make your own you will need:

◆ 2 tsps white vegetable fat
◆ 1 tsp liquid glucose
◆ 500 g/1 lb 2 oz royal icing
◆ 1 tbsp gum tragacanth
◆ 170 g/6 oz/1¼ c icing (confectioner's) sugar

1 Place the white fat and glucose in a mixing bowl over a pan of simmering water until melted.
2 Place the royal icing in a large mixing bowl, adding the gum tragacanth and the melted fat mixture and mix until it forms a paste. Gradually add the icing sugar, kneading the paste until it is smooth. Place the paste in an airtight container and refrigerate for 24 hours before using.

SUGAR PASTE

All the cakes in this book are covered with commercially manufactured sugar paste. However, you can make your own by following the recipe below.

◆ 3 tsps of albumen powder mixed with 90 ml/3 fl oz cold water **or** 1 medium egg white (due to the slight risk of salmonella it is advisable to use albumen powder)
◆ 2 tbsps liquid glucose
◆ 500 g/1 lb 2 oz/3¼ c icing (confectioner's) sugar

Add the albumen mix or egg white to the liquid glucose then gradually sift in the icing sugar, mixing all the time.

Colouring sugar paste

Sugar paste can be bought pre-coloured in a wide range of colours. If you cannot find the exact colour you need, you can buy uncoloured (white) sugar paste and colour it yourself with food colouring which you should add

gradually until the desired colour is achieved. When colouring small quantities of sugar paste, use a cocktail stick to add the food colouring to the paste. Do not be tempted to use too much colouring at a time as you can always add but not take away. Knead the paste until the colour is evenly distributed. Cut the paste in half and if there is still marbling, knead a little longer. Set aside to rest for a couple of hours before using.

FLOWER PASTE

(also known as gum paste and petal paste)
◆ 500 g/1 lb 2 oz/3¼ c icing (confectioner's) sugar
◆ 3 tsps gum tragacanth
◆ 5 tsps cold water
◆ 2 tsps powdered gelatine
◆ 2 tsps liquid glucose
◆ 3 tsp white vegetable fat
◆ 1 medium egg white (string removed)

1 Sieve the icing sugar and gum tragacanth together into a heavy-duty mixing bowl and set aside.
2 In a heatproof bowl, mix the water and the gelatine together and leave to stand for 30 minutes. Place the bowl over a saucepan of hot water, stirring with a fork to melt the gelatine. Add the glucose and white fat into the gelatine mix and heat gently until all the ingredients have melted and are mixed together.

3 Add all these ingredients to the icing sugar and gum tragacanth along with the egg white and beat on a low speed. When all the ingredients are amalgamated, increase the speed until the paste comes away from the side of the bowl.
4 Place the paste onto a board coated with white fat and knead gently until smooth. Double wrap in cling film and refrigerate for 24 hours before using.

Colouring flower paste

Flower paste can be coloured in the same way as sugar paste.

MODELLING PASTE

Commercial ready-made modelling paste is just as good but you can make your own by using a mixture of 50 per cent sugar paste and 50 per cent flower paste.

Colouring modelling paste

Modelling paste can be coloured in the same way as sugar paste.

MARZIPAN

Commercial marzipan is excellent both for covering cakes and for modelling, and I would not consider making it myself.

Colouring marzipan

Marzipan can be coloured in the same way as sugar paste.

COLOURED SUGARS

Coloured sugars are used mainly for decoration purposes and to add colour to cakes. Add four or five drops of food colouring to a jam jar containing 50 g/2 oz/⅓ c of caster sugar and shake vigorously for two to three minutes until the sugar is evenly coloured.

Sealed with a kiss

Lips and kisses are the theme for this cake and, linked together with its heart shape, it makes a great cake for Valentine's day or maybe an engagement.

YOU WILL NEED

- 21-cm (8-in) heart-shaped sponge cake (see p 12)
- 800 g (1 lb 12 oz) white sugar paste (see p 13)
- 300 g (10½ oz) raspberry or strawberry jam
- 500 g (1 lb 2 oz) buttercream (see p 12)
- 100 g (3½ oz) white royal icing (see p 12)
- 400 g (14 oz) red sugar paste (see p 13)

- Red food colouring
- 50 g (2 oz) royal icing coloured red (see p 12)
- Icing (confectioner's) sugar in a sugar shaker

EQUIPMENT

- Large non-stick rolling pin
- 30-cm (12-in) heart-shaped drum board
- Pastry brush

- Cake smoother
- Small sharp knife
- Large sharp knife
- Palette knife
- Spare board
- Piping bags
- Nos. 1 and 5 piping nozzles
- Red ribbon to finish the drum board

1 Roll out approximately 150 g (5½ oz) of the white sugar paste with the non-stick rolling pin so that it is large enough to cover the heart-shaped drum board. Using the pastry brush, dampen the board with water and cover it with the rolled out sugar paste. Smooth and polish the surface with the cake smoother. Trim off the excess with the small sharp knife and set aside to dry for a couple of hours.

2 Using the large sharp knife, level the top of the cake then cut it in half horizontally. With the palette knife, spread one half with jam and the other half with buttercream, keeping a little aside to thinly coat

the cake. Sandwich the two halves together and place upside down onto the spare board. Coat the top and sides of the cake with the remaining buttercream. Roll out the remaining white sugar paste so that it is large enough to cover the top and sides of the cake. Cover and smooth the cake as shown on pages 8–9, taking care to retain the shape of the cake. Set aside to dry for about 2 hours then place in the centre of the covered drum board.

3 Using the white royal icing and the No. 5 piping nozzle, pipe shells around the base of the cake to hide the join.

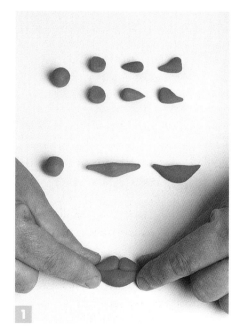

1

Making the lips

4 You will need 18 to 20 sets of lips. Use 20 g (¾ oz) of red sugar paste for each set of lips. Divide the quantity in two. To make the top lip, roll half the sugar paste into a ball and cut it in half. Take one half and roll it into a ball, then into a teardrop shape and flatten. Repeat with the other half of the ball and then press the two halves together at the large end to form a pout (*see pic 1*).

5 To make the lower lip, shape the remaining sugar paste as shown in the picture. Press the bottom and top lips together.

6 Secure the lips to the top and sides of the cake and the drum board with cooled boiled water. Finish off the cake with sets of kisses using red royal icing and the No. 1 piping nozzle (*see pic 2*). Finally, decorate the edge of the drum board with red ribbon.

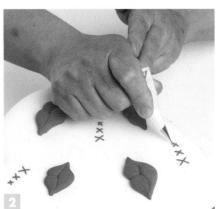

Piping sets of kisses

Some like it hot

This cake is on fire! The edible flames lap the sides of the cake to make an inferno topped off with a ring of flames bursting from the centre.

YOU WILL NEED

- 21-cm (8-in) round fruit cake (see p 11)
- 150 g (5½ oz) red sugar paste (see p 13)
- Apricot glaze (see p 12)
- 1 kg (2 lb 3 oz) marzipan
- 1 kg (2 lb 3 oz) white sugar paste (see p 13)
- Cornflour (cornstarch), for dusting
- Red, orange and yellow food colouring
- 200 g (7 oz) modelling paste coloured red (see p 13)

- 200 g (7 oz) modelling paste coloured orange (see p 13)
- 200 g (7 oz) modelling paste coloured yellow (see p 13)
- 50 g (2 oz) royal icing (see p 12)
- Icing (confectioner's) sugar in a sugar shaker

EQUIPMENT

- Large and small non-stick rolling pins
- 28-cm (11-in) round drum board

- Pastry brush
- Cake smoother
- Small sharp knife
- Large sharp knife
- Spare board
- Craft knife
- Sponge for drying
- Red ribbon to finish the drum board

1 Roll out the red sugar paste with the non-stick rolling pin so that it is large enough to cover the round drum board. Using the pastry brush, dampen the board with water and cover it with the rolled out sugar paste. Smooth and polish the surface with the cake smoother. Trim off the excess with the small sharp knife and set aside to dry for a couple of hours.

2 Using the large sharp knife, level the top of the cake, turn it upside down and place it on the spare board. Brush the top and sides with apricot glaze. Roll out the marzipan so that it is large enough to cover the top and sides of the cake. Cover and smooth

the cake as shown on pages 8–9. Set aside to dry for about 2 hours.

3 Roll out the white sugar paste, brush the marzipan with cooled boiled water and cover the top and sides with the sugar paste, using the method on page 9. Trim off the excess. Leave to dry for about 2 hours then place the cake in the centre of the covered drum board.

4 Using the small non-stick rolling pin, thinly roll out the red modelling paste onto a board lightly dusted with cornflour. With the craft knife, cut out random flame shapes and sizes and

Cutting out the flames

place them on a piece of sponge to dry. Make sure the base of the flames is straight as they have to sit on the drum board. Repeat with the orange and yellow modelling pastes (*see pic 1*). Turn the flames over after 12 hours to allow them to dry on both sides.

5 When the flames are dry, stick them randomly to the side of the cake with a dab of royal icing (*see pic 2*). Make sure you keep some flames aside for the top piece of the cake.

6 To make the top piece, mould a spare piece of white sugar paste into a cylinder 5-cm (2-in) in diameter and 2½-cm (1-in) high and leave to harden. Fit the remaining flame shapes around the cylinder attaching them with royal icing and leave to dry then stick the top piece on the centre of

Making the top piece

the cake with royal icing (*see pic 3*). Finally, decorate the edge of the drum board with red ribbon.

Sticking down the flames

Pinks and pearls

This two-tier cake is a delightful alternative cake for a small wedding. The colours can be altered to match the bride's colour scheme.

YOU WILL NEED

- 25-cm (10-in) square fruit cake (see p 11)
- 15-cm (6-in) square fruit cake (see p 11)
- 2 kg (4 lb 6 oz) pink sugar paste (see p 13)
- Apricot glaze (see p 12)
- 3 kg (6 lb 10 oz) marzipan
- 1 kg (2 lb 3 oz) ivory sugar paste (see p 13)
- Ivory and pink food colouring
- 75 g (2½ oz) royal icing coloured ivory (see p 12)
- 75 g (2½ oz) royal icing coloured pink (see p 12)
- Icing (confectioner's) sugar in a sugar shaker

EQUIPMENT

- Large non-stick rolling pin
- 36-cm (14-in) square drum board

- Pastry brush
- Cake smoother
- Small sharp knife
- Large sharp knife
- Spare board
- 15-cm (6-in) square hard board
- 3 dowels
- Piping bags
- Nos. 3 and 4 piping nozzles
- Fine paintbrush
- Ivory ribbon to finish the drum board
- 20 silver wires
- Approx 288 ivory pearl beads
- Fine pliers
- 7 pink pearl beads
- Strong glue
- 2 food-grade flower picks

1 Roll out approximately 175 g (6 oz) of the pink sugar paste with the non-stick rolling pin so that it is large enough to cover the square drum board. Using the pastry brush, dampen the board with water and cover it with the rolled out sugar paste. Smooth and polish the surface with the cake smoother. Trim off the excess with the small sharp knife and set aside to dry for a couple of hours.

2 Using the large sharp knife, level the top of each cake, turn them upside down and place the larger cake onto the spare board and the smaller one onto the hard board of the same size. Brush the top and sides of the cakes with apricot glaze. Roll out the marzipan so that it is large enough to cover the top and sides of each cake. Cover and smooth the cakes as shown on pages 8–9. Set aside to dry for about 12 hours.

3 Roll out the remaining pink sugar paste, brush the marzipan with cooled boiled water and cover the top and sides of the larger cake with the sugar paste, using the method on page 9. Trim off the excess. Leave to dry for about 2 hours then place the bottom cake in the centre of the covered drum board. While it is still soft, emboss it randomly using a pearl butterfly (see Steps 6 and 7). Dowel the bottom tier as shown on page 10.

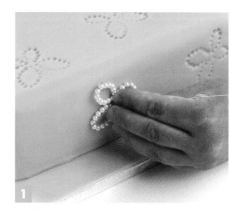

Embossing the cake

Cover the smaller cake and the hard board in ivory sugar paste and emboss as for the bottom tier.

4 Using the No. 3 piping nozzle and the ivory-coloured royal icing, dot the embossed butterfly design on the lower tier (*see pic 2*). Use a fine, slightly damp paintbrush to soften the tips of the peaks. When dry, place the top tier centrally over the bottom tier and repeat the process on the top tier, but this time using pink-coloured royal icing.

Piping the dot design to hide the join

Dotting the design

5 Using the No. 4 piping nozzle and contrasting-coloured royal icing, pipe a dot design between the join of the bottom cake and the board then between the join of the stacked cakes (*see pic 3*). Decorate the edge of the drum board with ivory ribbon.

6 To make the butterflies (you will need 6 in total) you will need two silver wires and 48 ivory pearl beads per butterfly. Slightly bend a silver wire 7 cm (3 in) from one end with the pliers to prevent the threaded pearls from dropping off the wire then thread 13 ivory pearl beads to form the top wing shape and secure in a loop by twisting the wire. Then thread 10 pearls onto the same wire and twist again to form the bottom wing. Repeat the process for the other side of the

Making the butterflies

wing. Join the two sides together and twist the long wires in the centre to join them then cut away one of the wires close to the twist. Twist the remaining wire around a pencil to give it a spring shape (*see pic 4*).

7 To make the body, thread two pearl beads onto one of the 7-cm (3-in) wires left on the other end and twist to secure in place. Twist the two spare pieces of wire to make the butterfly's antennae. Finally, stick a single pearl bead at the tip of each antenna with a little glue (*see pic 5*).

8 To make the single pink pearl decorations (you will seven in total), thread a single pearl onto the end of a silver wire, securing with a dab of glue, then wrap the wire around a pencil to achieve a spring-like shape (*see pic 6*).

5

Assembling the butterflies

6

Coiling the wire around the pencil

9 Insert a flower pick into the centre of the top cake and place five butterflies and five pink pearl wires into it. Insert another flower pick into one of the bottom corners of the top cake and place one butterfly and two pink pearl wires into it. If the wires feel lose in the pick, fill it with sugar paste the same colour as the cake covering (*see pic 7*).

7

Positioning the decorations

Babe in the woods

The design of this cake allows the baby to nestle in a bed of leaves hidden in the forest.

YOU WILL NEED

- 21-cm (8-in) oval fruit cake (use recipe for 8-in round cake p 11)
- 1.1 kg (2 lb 7 oz) pale green sugar paste (see p 13)
- Apricot glaze (see p 12)
- 1.1 kg (2 lb 7 oz) marzipan
- Brown, green and flesh food colouring
- 150 g (5½ oz) flower paste coloured green (see p 13)
- 100 g (3½ oz) brown sugar paste (see p 13)

- 50 g (2 oz) royal icing (see p 12)
- Icing (confectioner's) sugar in a sugar shaker

EQUIPMENT

- Large and small non-stick rolling pins
- 30-cm (12-in) oval drum board
- Pastry brush
- Cake smoother

- Small sharp knife
- Large sharp knife
- Spare board
- Craft knife
- Sponge for drying
- Metal sieve
- Fine paintbrush
- Pale green ribbon to finish the drum board

1 Roll out approximately 150 g (5½ oz) of the pale green sugar paste with the non-stick rolling pin so that it is large enough to cover the oval drum board. Using the pastry brush, dampen the board with water and cover it with the rolled out sugar paste. Smooth and polish the surface with the cake smoother. Trim off the excess with the small sharp knife and set aside to dry for a couple of hours.

2 Using the large sharp knife, level the top of the cake, turn it upside down and place it onto the spare board. Brush the top and sides with apricot glaze. Roll out 1 kg (2 lb 3 oz) of marzipan so that it is large enough to cover the top and sides of the cake. Cover and smooth the cake as shown on pages 8–9. Set aside to dry for about 2 hours.

3 Roll out the remaining pale green sugar paste, brush the marzipan with cooled boiled water and cover the top and sides with the sugar paste,

using the method on page 9. Trim off the excess. Leave to dry for about 2 hours then place the cake in the centre of the covered drum board.

4 Copy the tree top template on page 78 and cut it out. Roll out the green flower paste, place the

template on top and cut around it using the craft knife. Cut out five more tree tops. Next, cut out 15 leaf shapes of various sizes, lightly score them lengthways and bend them slightly to give them movement (see pic 1). Place the tree tops and leaves on a piece of sponge to firm up.

1

Cutting out the tree tops

5 To make the three mushrooms, use 50 g (2 oz) of the brown sugar paste and divide it into six equal portions. Roll three portions into walnut-size balls then shape them so that they are slightly pointy on top and flat at the bottom. Make stumps with the remaining three portions and stick them to the base of the mushrooms with a little water. Set aside to dry. Copy the trunk template on page 78 and cut it out. Roll out the remaining brown sugar paste, place the template on top and cut around it. You will need six in total. Attach these to the side of the cake at equal intervals with cooled boiled water then attach the tree tops with royal icing (*see pic 2*).

Attaching the tree tops

6 Add a few drops of green food colouring to spare pale green sugar paste and soften it with a little water. Push it through the sieve with the back of a spoon to create a grass effect. Scrape it off with the craft knife and attach it around the base, using a little water to stick it down. Place a few tufts on top of the cake too (*see pic 3*).

Making the grass

Positioning the leaves

7 When the leaves have dried, place them on top of the cake to create a bed of leaves on which the baby will lie. Attach them with a little royal icing (*see pic 4*).

8 To make the baby, colour the remaining marzipan a skin colour. Make the various body parts as shown below. Using 50 g (2 oz) of marzipan for the torso, make the remaining body parts so that they are in proportion with the torso (*see pic 5*). Stick the pieces together with water and place the baby, belly down, on the bed of leaves. Paint in the eyes and mouth using the paintbrush and the brown food colouring and use a tiny piece of brown sugar paste to make a tuft of hair. Stick the mushrooms on the top of the cake with a little water. Finally, decorate the edge of the drum board with pale green ribbon.

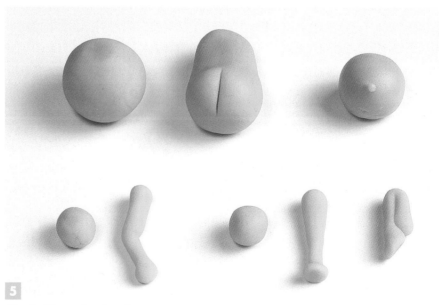

Modelling the body parts

Roman column

This three-tier cake would make a wedding cake with a difference. The grapes can be changed for flowers to match your theme.

YOU WILL NEED

- Three 21-cm (8-in) round fruit cakes (see p 11)
- 3 kg (6 lb 10 oz) white sugar paste (see p 13)
- 100 g (3½ oz) royal icing (see p 12)
- Apricot glaze (see p 12)
- 2¾ kg (6 lb 2 oz) marzipan, for covering the cakes
- Glycerine
- Sugar glue (see p 12)
- 50 g (2 oz) flower paste (see p 13)
- Gold dust
- Isopropohyl alcohol

- Purple and brown food colouring
- 600 g (1 lb 5 oz) marzipan, for decoration
- Icing (confectioner's) sugar in a sugar shaker

EQUIPMENT

- Two 30-cm (12-in) round drum boards
- Two 25-cm (10-in) round drum boards
- Double-sided sticky tape
- Large and small non-stick rolling pins
- Pastry brush

- Cake smoother
- Small sharp knife
- Large sharp knife
- Spare board
- Two 21-cm (8-in) round hard boards
- Sugarcraft gun fitted with large trefoil-shaped disc
- Eight 26-g white wires
- Small leaf cutter
- Sponge for drying
- Fine paintbrush
- White florist tape
- White ribbon to finish the drum board

1 Stick the smaller drum board centrally on top of the larger one with double-sided sticky tape. Repeat for the other set of drum boards. Roll out approximately 200 g (7 oz) of the white sugar paste with the non-stick rolling pin so that it is large enough to cover the stacked drum boards. Using the pastry brush, dampen the boards with water and cover them with the rolled out sugar paste. Smooth and polish the surface with the cake smoother. Trim off the excess with the small sharp knife and set aside to dry for a couple of hours. Repeat for the other stacked boards.

2 Using the large sharp knife, level the top of each cake, turn them upside down and place one onto a spare board. Place a hard board of the same size as the cake on top, securing with royal icing. Stack the

second cake on top and place another hard board over it, again securing with royal icing. Lastly, place the third cake on top so that you have three stacked cakes.

Covering with marzipan

3 Brush the top and sides of the cakes with apricot glaze. Roll out the marzipan so that it is wide and long enough to wrap around the sides

of all three stacked cakes, keeping a piece aside for the top. Cover and smooth the sides as shown on pages 8–9. Now roll out the remaining marzipan and cover the top of the cake, trimming off the excess with the small sharp knife (see pic 1). Set aside to dry for about 12 hours.

4 Roll out the remaining white sugar paste so that it is wide and long enough to wrap around the sides of all three cakes. Brush the marzipan with cooled boiled water and cover the sides with the sugar paste until the edges meet. You may find it easier to roll up the sugar paste then wrap it around the sides like a bandage (see pic 2). Take extra care with the join which should be smoothed with the cake smoother until almost invisible. Leave to dry for about 24 hours then place the stacked cakes centrally onto one of the covered drum boards, using royal icing to stick it down. Place the other covered drum board on top of the stacked cakes, securing again with royal icing. The underside of the top drum board is then covered with sugar paste. Set aside for 24 hours until the royal icing has set the cakes to the boards.

2

Covering with sugar paste

5 Using gold dust mixed with a few drops of isopropyl alcohol, paint in the marble effect on the column (*see pic 3*).

6 Fill any gaps at the base of the cake with softened white sugar paste. Fill the sugarcraft gun with sugar paste rendered down with a few drops of glycerine and make a rope for the base of the cake. Stick it in place with sugar glue (*see pic 4*). Make a second rope for the top of the column and stick it in place. This is

5

Making and assembling the olive leaves

tricky so turn the column upside down and secure it this way. Take care when turning the cake over as it is very heavy.

7 To make the olive leaves, cut the wires into thirds. Thinly roll out the flower paste leaving a thin ridge of thicker paste in the centre. Stamp out a leaf keeping the ridge in the centre of the leaf cutter. You will need 22 leaves in total. Brush the end of the wire with sugar glue and push it into the ridge of the leaf. Secure the wire into the paste and gently shape the leaf to give it some movement. Leave to harden on a piece of sponge then paint with gold dust mixed with a few drops of isopropyl alcohol. Repeat for each leaf then tape them together with white florist tape, painting over the

tape with the gold dust mixture (*see pic 5*). Shape the headdress by gently bending it into a semi circle. Refer to Steps 7 to 9 on page 69 to make the ivy leaves.

8 Set aside 50 g (2 oz) of the marzipan for decoration. Colour the remainder purple and roll 10-g (⅓-oz) balls for each grape then shape into ovals. You will need two bunches and each bunch has about 25 grapes. Model the grapes straight onto the top and bottom of the column and stick them down with water (*see pic 6*). Colour the set aside marzipan brown and shape it into stalks and place a stalk on each bunch. Finally, decorate the edges of the top and bottom drum boards with white ribbon.

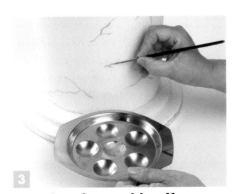

3

Creating the marble effect

4

Sticking down the rope

6

Positioning the grapes

Art decodence

The style and pure over-indulgence of this period shows through in this cake. The fan design and feathers represent the period perfectly.

YOU WILL NEED

- 21-cm (8-in) square fruit cake (see p 11)
- Blue, green and black food colouring
- 225 g (8 oz) black sugar paste (see p 13)
- Apricot glaze (see p 12)
- 1.1 kg (2 lb 7 oz) marzipan
- 1 kg (2 lb 3 oz) turquoise sugar paste (see p 13)
- 500 g (1 lb 2 oz) white royal icing (see p 12)
- Gold and silver dusts
- Isopropohyl alcohol
- Icing (confectioner's) sugar in a sugar shaker

EQUIPMENT

- Large non-stick rolling pin
- 28-cm (11-in) square drum board
- Pastry brush
- Cake smoother
- Small sharp knife
- Large sharp knife
- Four spare boards
- Piping bags
- Nos. 1.5, 3 and 5 piping nozzles
- Fine paintbrush
- Low tack tape
- Cellophane wrap
- Crank palette knife
- 12 black feathers
- Round cutter 3-cm (1¼-in) in diameter
- Sponge for drying
- Black ribbon to finish the drum board

1 If you cannot get hold of turquoise sugar paste, you can mix the colour yourself by colouring white sugar paste with a mix of blue and green food colouring. Once you have achieved the right colour, set it aside to rest for a couple of hours before using. Roll out approximately 150 g (5½ oz) of the black sugar paste with the non-stick rolling pin so that it is large enough to cover the square drum board. Using the pastry brush, dampen the board with water and cover it with the rolled out sugar paste. Smooth and polish the surface with the cake smoother. Trim off the excess with the small sharp knife and set aside to dry for a couple of hours.

2 Using the large sharp knife, level the top of the cake, turn it upside down and place it on a spare board. Brush the top and sides with apricot glaze. Roll out the marzipan so that it is large enough to cover the top and sides of the cake. Cover and smooth the cake as shown on pages 8–9. Set aside to dry for about 2 hours.

3 Roll out the turquoise sugar paste, brush the marzipan with cooled boiled water and cover the top and sides with the sugar paste, using the method on page 9. Trim off the excess. Leave to dry for about 2 hours then place the cake in the centre of the covered drum board.

4 Copy the fan template on page 78, cut it out and scratch the design onto the top of the cake using a pin. With the No. 1.5 piping nozzle, outline the pattern with white royal icing (*see pic 1*). When the royal icing has hardened, carefully paint it with gold and silver dust mixed with a few drops of isopropyl alcohol. Set aside to dry.

5 In the meantime, make the side decorations. Secure four fan designs from page 78 with low tack tape to a spare board large enough

Outlining the pattern with royal icing

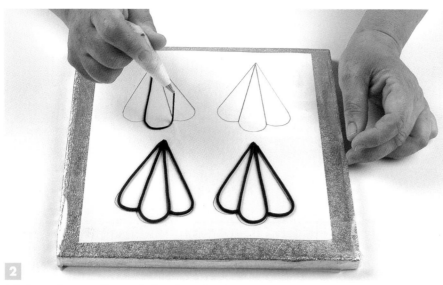

2

Piping the outline of the fan designs

to hold all four fan designs. You need three fan designs per side, so 12 in total (and therefore three spare boards). Place cellophane wrap tightly over the pattern and secure in place with low tack tape. Colour a little royal icing with black food colouring and, using the No. 3 piping nozzle, pipe the outline of the design (*see pic 2*). Take care to join all the lines so that there are no gaps. Smooth down any take-off lines with a damp paintbrush and leave to dry until hard.

6 Water down the remaining white royal icing until it is of a flowing consistency. Place it in a piping bag and cut a small hole in the bottom of the bag. Flood the run outs with the thinned royal icing making sure to

not overfill (*see pic 3*). Gently tap the board to level the icing. Dry uncovered under a lamp for about 6 hours to help keep the sheen then move to a warm place, uncovered, for a further 48 hours.

7 When the run outs have hardened, paint the fans using gold and silver dusts mixed with a few drops of isopropyl alcohol. When dry, gently remove the fans from the board with a crank palette knife. Stick a feather to the back of each fan with

a dab of royal icing and secure three fans onto each side of the cake, placing a piece of cellophane between the cake and the feathers so that the feathers are not in direct contact with the cake (*see pic 4*).

8 Cut out five circles out of the remaining black sugar paste, cutting a small slice off four of the circles. Leave to dry on a piece of sponge. Then, with royal icing, stick the cut black circles at the bottom of the fans where the tips meet and place the full circle centrally onto the top of the cake (*see pic 5*). Finally, decorate the edge of the drum board with black ribbon.

5

Sticking down the circles

3

Flooding the run outs

4

Securing the fans to the sides of the cake

House of cards

This square cake is ideal for a man's birthday. The cards around the sides of the cake could add up to the age of the birthday boy in question.

YOU WILL NEED

- 500 g (1 lb 2 oz) pastillage (see p 13)
- Icing (confectioner's) sugar in a sugar shaker
- 1.1 kg (2 lb 7 oz) white sugar paste (see p 13)
- 21-cm (8-in) square fruit cake (see p 11)
- Apricot glaze (see p 12)
- 1.1 kg (2 lb 7 oz) marzipan
- Sugar glue (see p 12)
- Black and red food colouring
- 225 g (8 oz) blue sugar paste (see p 13)
- 50 g (2 oz) flower paste coloured red (see page 13)

- 50 g (2 oz) flower paste coloured black (see page 13)
- 50 g (2 oz) red royal icing (see p 12)
- 50 g (2 oz) black royal icing (see p 12)
- 110 g (4 oz) white royal icing (see p 12)

EQUIPMENT

- Large and small non-stick rolling pins
- Non-stick board
- Card cutter
- Sponge for drying
- Small palette knife

- 28-cm (11-in) square drum board
- Pastry brush
- Cake smoother
- Small sharp knife
- Large sharp knife
- Spare board
- Firm piece of sponge
- Star-patterned roller
- Card suit cutters (hearts, clubs, diamonds and spades)
- Fine paintbrush
- Piping bags
- Nos. 1 and 3 piping nozzles
- White ribbon to finish the drum board

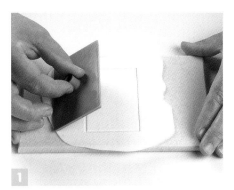

1

Stamping out the card shapes

2 Roll out approximately 150 g (5½ oz) of the white sugar paste with the large non-stick rolling pin so that it is large enough to cover the square drum board. Using the pastry brush, dampen the board with water and cover it with the rolled out sugar paste. Smooth and polish the surface with the cake smoother. Trim off the excess with the small sharp knife and set aside to dry for a couple of hours.

4 Roll out the remaining white sugar paste, brush the marzipan with cooled boiled water and cover the top and sides with the sugar paste, using the method on page 9. Trim off the excess. Leave to dry for about 2 hours then place the cake in the centre of the covered drum board.

1 Using the small non-stick rolling pin, thinly roll out the pastillage on a non-stick board dusted with icing sugar. Using the card cutter, stamp out 22 card shapes (12 for the sides and 10 for the top) and leave to dry flat on a piece of sponge for 24 hours before turning and leaving for a further 24 hours (*see pic 1*). Use the small palette knife when placing the cards on the sponge and take care not to distort the shapes.

3 Using the large sharp knife, level the top of the cake, turn it upside down and place it onto the spare board. Brush the top and sides with apricot glaze. Roll out the marzipan so that it is large enough to cover the top and sides of the cake. Cover and smooth the cake as shown on pages 8–9. Set aside to dry for about 2 hours.

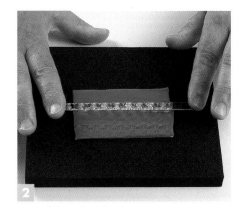

2

Marking in the pattern

3

Sticking down the suit shapes

4

Piping the shell to hide the join

5 When the card shapes have hardened, brush the back of each card with sugar glue and then cover with a thin layer of blue sugar paste. Place the card, sugar paste-up, onto a firm piece of sponge and gently roll the star-patterned rolling pin over it to mark in the pattern (*see pic 2*). Take care when doing this as pastillage is fragile and can snap easily. Set aside to dry for 1 hour.

6 Roll out the red and black flower pastes and stamp out suit shapes using the card suit cutters then set aside to dry on a piece of sponge. When the backs are dry, stick the cut-out shapes onto the front of each card with a little sugar glue (*see pic 3*). Using the No. 1 piping nozzle, pipe the numbers in each corner of the cards in red and back royal icing.

7 With white royal icing and the No. 3 piping nozzle, pipe a small shell around the base of the cake to hide the join (*see pic 4*). With the help of a little royal icing on the back

of each card, attach three cards to each side of the cake while the shell around the base is still soft. Alternate the colours around the cake, as shown in the picture.

8 Make the house of cards for the top of the cake (*see pic 5*). Using the No. 3 piping nozzle, pipe a fine line of royal icing on the edge of the cards to glue them together. Take care to remove any excess royal icing at the joins with a small dampened paintbrush. Leave the cake to dry completely before moving it. Finally, decorate the edge of the drum board with white ribbon.

5

Building the house of cards

Out of this world

Planets and zodiac signs are the decorations for this cake. It is simple yet very effective and makes an ideal cake for any child's birthday.

YOU WILL NEED

- 21-cm (8-in) round sponge cake (see p 12)
- 800 g (1 lb 12 oz) purple sugar paste (see p 13)
- 300 g (10½ oz) raspberry or strawberry jam
- 500 g (1 lb 2 oz) buttercream (see p 12)
- 75 g (2½ oz) each of green, pink and blue sugar paste (see p 13)
- Purple food colouring
- 100 g (3½ oz) royal icing coloured purple (see p 12)

- Gold dust
- Isopropyl alcohol
- Icing (confectioner's) sugar in a sugar shaker

EQUIPMENT
- Large and small non-stick rolling pins
- 28-cm (11-in) round drum board
- Pastry brush
- Cake smoother

- Small sharp knife
- Large sharp knife
- Palette knife
- Spare board
- Round cutters in various sizes
- Sponge for drying
- 1 m (39 in) gold cord
- Piping bag
- No. 1 piping nozzle
- Fine paintbrush
- Purple ribbon to finish the drum board

1 Roll out approximately 150 g (5½ oz) of the purple sugar paste with the non-stick rolling pin so that it is large enough to cover the round drum board. Using the pastry brush, dampen the board with water and cover it with the rolled out sugar paste. Smooth and polish the surface with the cake smoother. Trim off the excess with the small sharp knife and set aside to dry for a couple of hours.

2 Using the large sharp knife, level the top of the cake then cut it in half horizontally. With the palette knife, spread one half with jam and the other half with buttercream, keeping a little aside to thinly coat the cake. Sandwich the two halves together and place upside down onto the spare board. Coat the top and sides of the cake with the remaining buttercream. Roll out the remaining purple sugar paste so that it is large enough to cover the top and sides of the cake. Cover and smooth the cake as shown on pages 8–9. Set aside to dry for about 2 hours then place in the centre of the covered drum board.

3 Using the three coloured sugar pastes, stamp out 10 circles of various sizes: these will be the planets. Leave three circles (one of each colour) to dry flat on a piece of sponge.

4 Using smaller circular cutters, cut out random circles from some of the larger base circles and substitute them with a different colour (*see pic 1*). Using cooled boiled water, stick some of the planets around the side of the cake. Finish the top of the cake with three dried planets, attaching them with a little royal icing.

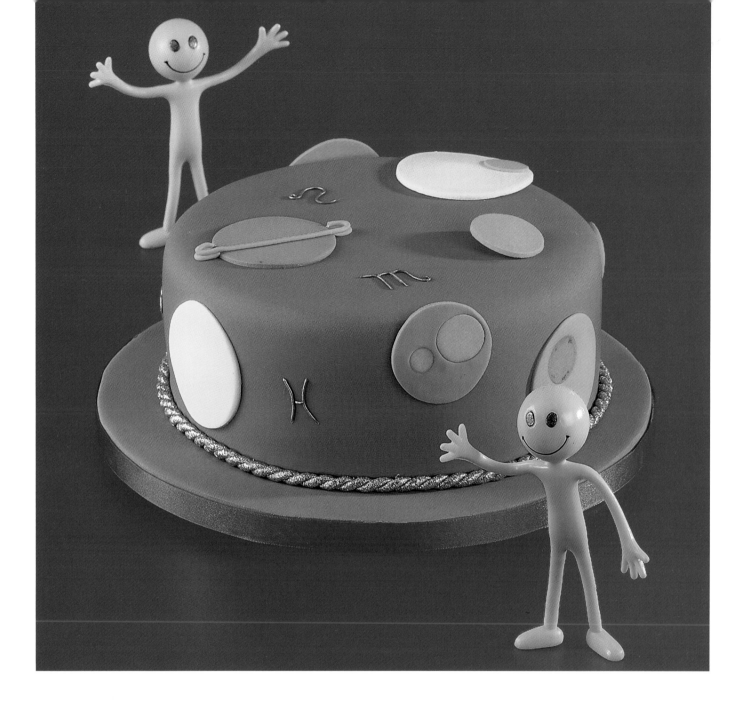

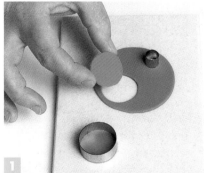

1

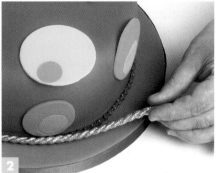

2

3

Cutting out circles

Decorating the base of the cake

Painting the zodiac signs

5 Attach the gold cord around the base of the cake with a little royal icing (*see pic 2*). Using the No. 1 piping nozzle and purple coloured

royal icing thinned with a little water, randomly pipe zodiac signs (*see page 78*) around the cake, painting them with gold dust mixed

with a few drops of isopropyl alcohol when dry (*see pic 3*). Finish by decorating the edge of the drum board with purple ribbon.

A walk on the wild side

Each tier of this cake is wrapped with a drape of tiger-patterned sugar paste. The pattern of the drape can be changed to any design of your choice.

YOU WILL NEED

- 25-cm (10-in) round fruit cake (see p 11)
- 21-cm (8-in) round fruit cake (see p 11)
- 15-cm (6-in) round fruit cake (see p 11)
- 4 kg (8 lb 13 oz) white sugar paste (see p 13)
- Apricot glaze (see p 12)
- 4 kg (8 lb 13 oz) marzipan
- 225 g (8 oz) white royal icing (see p 12)

- 2 kg (4 lb 6 oz) orange sugar paste (see p 13)
- 225 g (8 oz) black sugar paste (see p 13)
- Icing (confectioner's) sugar in a sugar shaker

EQUIPMENT

- Large non-stick rolling pin
- 36-cm (14-in) round drum board
- Pastry brush
- Cake smoother

- Small sharp knife
- Large sharp knife
- Spare board
- 21-cm (8-in) round hard board
- 15-cm (6-in) round hard board
- Six dowels
- Piping bags
- No. 5 piping nozzle
- Fabric texture roller
- White ribbon to finish the drum board

1 Roll out approximately 175 g (6 oz) of the white sugar paste with the non-stick rolling pin so that it is large enough to cover the round drum board. Using the pastry brush, dampen the board with water and cover it with the rolled out sugar paste. Smooth and polish the surface with the cake smoother. Trim off the excess with the small sharp knife and set aside to dry for a couple of hours.

2 Using the large sharp knife, level the top of each cake, turn them upside down and place the largest cake onto the spare board and the other two onto hard boards of the same size. Brush the top and sides of the cakes with apricot glaze. Roll out the marzipan so that it is large enough to cover the top and sides of each cake. Cover and smooth the cakes as shown on pages 8–9. Set aside to dry for about 12 hours.

3 Roll out the remaining white sugar paste, brush the marzipan with cooled boiled water and cover the top and sides of each cake with the sugar paste, using the method on page 9. Trim off the excess. Leave to dry for about 2 hours. Place the largest cake in the centre of the covered drum board. Dowel the bottom two tiers as shown on page 10, using a little royal icing to stick each tier together. With white royal icing and the No. 5 piping nozzle, pipe a small shell around the base of each tier to hide the join.

4 To make the rosette at the top of the cake, roll out 50 g (2 oz) of the orange sugar paste. Cut out strips of black sugar paste and place them over the orange strip, using the fabric texture roller to embed them into the sugar paste. Cut into a 17 x 30-cm (7 x 12-in) strip. Fold the strip in half lengthways and gather the edges into the centre. Keep adding strips to form the rosette on top of the cake. Set aside to dry for a couple of hours (*see pic 1*).

Forming the rosette

5 To make the drape, roll out the remaining orange sugar paste into three 30 x 20-cm (12 x 8-in) strips and make black markings as with the rosette (*see pic 2*). Starting from the bottom, drape the first strip half way around the bottom tier so that it looks like a fabric drape, sticking it down with cooled boiled water (*see pic 3*). Place the end of the second strip over the edge of the first to hide the join and drape around the middle tier. Repeat with the third strip to the top of the cake. If the drape is too long, cut off any excess paste. Place the hardened rosette on the top tier to complete the cake (*see pic 4*). Finally, decorate the edge of the drum board with white ribbon.

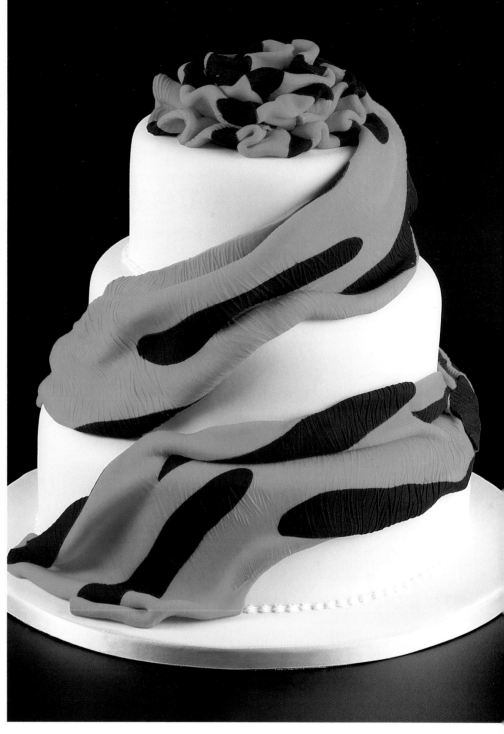

Making the drape

Sticking down the drape

Positioning the rosette

Poodle power

This pink fluffy cake will impress the party princess in your life. Ideal as a birthday cake for the pooch lovers among us!

YOU WILL NEED

- 21-cm (8-in) hexagonal fruit cake (use recipe for 8-in round cake p 11)
- 1 kg (2 lb 3 oz) white sugar paste (see p 13)
- Apricot glaze (see p 12)
- 1 kg (2 lb 3 oz) marzipan
- 500 g (1 lb 2 oz) white royal icing (see p 12)
- Pink and black food colouring
- 25 g (1 oz) pink coloured flower paste (see p 13)
- Icing (confectioner's) sugar in a sugar shaker

EQUIPMENT

- Large non-stick rolling pin
- 30-cm (12-in) hexagonal drum board
- Pastry brush
- Cake smoother
- Small sharp knife
- Large sharp knife
- Spare board
- Piping bags
- Nos. 1 and 5 piping nozzles
- Spare boards (for the run outs)
- Low tack tape
- Cellophane wrap
- Fine paintbrush
- Crank palette knife
- Small bow cutter
- White ribbon to finish the drum board
- 1 m (39 in) pink marabou fur

1 Roll out approximately 150 g (5½ oz) of the white sugar paste with the non-stick rolling pin so that it is large enough to cover the hexagonal drum board. Using the pastry brush, dampen the board with water and cover it with the rolled out sugar paste. Smooth and polish the surface with the cake smoother. Trim off the excess with the small sharp knife and set aside to dry for a couple of hours.

2 Using the large sharp knife, level the top of the cake, turn it upside down onto the spare board. Brush the top and sides of the cake with apricot glaze. Roll out the marzipan so that it is large enough to cover the top and sides of the cake. Cover and smooth the cake as shown on pages 8–9. Set aside to dry for about 2 hours.

3 Roll out the remaining white sugar paste, brush the marzipan with cooled boiled water and cover the top and sides with the sugar paste, using the method on page 9. Trim off the excess. Leave to dry for about 2 hours then place the cake in the centre of the covered drum board.

4 Using white royal icing and the No. 5 piping nozzle, pipe a shell border at the base of the cake to hide the join.

5 Photocopy the poodle template on page 79 and secure it to a spare board with low tack tape. Each board will fit about four poodles and you will need 10 to 12 in total. Place cellophane wrap tightly over the templates and secure in place with low tack tape. Colour most of the remaining royal icing (saving a small quantity for the contrasting colour) bright pink with a few drops of pink food colouring. Using the No. 1 piping nozzle, outline the poodles. Always use freshly-made royal icing for run outs to help prevent them sinking and also to give a better sheen. Take care to join all the lines so that there are no gaps. Smooth down any take-off lines with a damp paintbrush and leave to dry until hard. Save a small amount of bright pink royal icing as you will need more for the ears, fur, tails and legs and a colour match can be difficult to achieve.

6 With the No. 1 piping nozzle and the bright pink royal icing, pipe the ears and ball of fur on top of the head of each poodle. This gives a textured effect to the run out. Change the consistency of the royal icing by adding a little water until it is of a flowing consistency. Flood in the main body and head of each poodle (*see pic 1*). Leave to skim over then

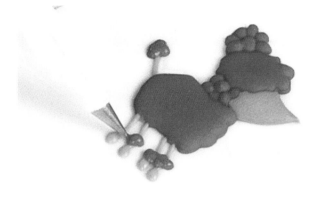

2

Adding the finishing touches

pale the colour down by adding some white royal icing set aside from Step 5 until you achieve the desired colour and run out the face. Tap the board lightly to level the icing. Dry uncovered under a lamp for about 6 hours to help keep the sheen then leave in a warm place, uncovered, for a further 48 hours. The strong colours of the icing may slow down the drying time.

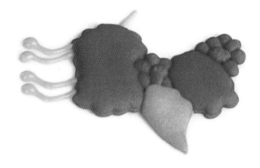

8 Cut out as may bow shapes as there are poodles from the pink flower paste using the bow cutter and secure to each poodle with a little royal icing (*see pic 3*). Decorate the edge of the drum board with white ribbon and finish by wrapping the fur around the base of the cake, ensuring there is a piece of cellophane between the cake and the fur.

1

Flooding in the head and body

7 When the run outs are dry, gently remove them from the board with a crank palette knife and secure them to the top of the cake with a dab of royal icing (*see pic 2*). Using a fine paintbrush, paint in the eyes and nose with black food colouring. Using pale pink royal icing and the No. 1 piping nozzle, pipe on the legs and tail. Pipe the end of the tail and ankles using the bright pink colour to create the tonal effect.

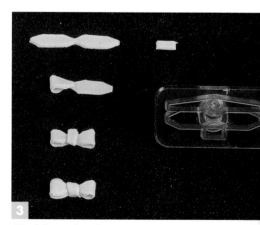

3

Making the bows

Beautiful butterflies

Keeping the covering and piping all one colour accentuates the pretty pastel butterflies on this cake. It makes a lovely birthday or retirement cake, or something a little special for the nature lovers among us.

YOU WILL NEED

- 100 g (3½ oz) flower paste (see p 13)
- Lustre dusts in pink, green, lilac, yellow, red and blue
- Isopropyl alcohol
- Black food colouring
- 250 g (9 oz) white royal icing (see p 12)
- 1½ kg (3 lb 5 oz) white sugar paste (see p 13)
- 25-cm (10-in) petal-shaped sponge cake (see p 12)
- 350 g (12½ oz) raspberry or strawberry jam

- 600 g (1 lb 5 oz) buttercream (see p 12)
- Icing (confectioner's) sugar in a sugar shaker

EQUIPMENT

- Large and small non-stick rolling pins
- Non-stick board
- Butterfly wing cutters in large, medium and small
- Sponge for drying
- Fine paintbrush
- Card and greaseproof paper

for butterfly supports
- Piping bags
- Nos. 2, 42 and 52 piping nozzles
- 36-cm (14-in) round drum board
- Pastry brush
- Cake smoother
- Small sharp knife
- Large sharp knife
- Palette knife
- Spare board
- Lilac ribbon to finish the drum board

1 Painting the wings

1 Start by making the butterflies. You will need 18 in total. Thinly roll out the flower paste on the non-stick board and stamp out six sets of wings from each of the three butterfly cutters. Dry the wings on a sponge until hard.

2 Mix the lustre dusts with a few drops of isopropyl alcohol to achieve a consistency that is thin enough to paint with. Remember, you can mix the dusts together to make different colours. Paint each butterfly in a pattern of your choice and paint in any black markings using the black food colouring (see pic 1). Set aside to dry.

3 Fold the card as shown in the picture to make a support for the butterflies and line it with greaseproof paper. Place two wings of the same size side by side and, using the No. 2 piping nozzle and white royal icing, pipe a fine line down the centre to stick the wings together. When dry,

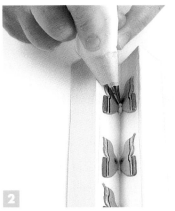

2

Joining the wings together

pipe small decorative dots over the join to form the body (*see pic 2*).

4 Roll out approximately 175 g (6 oz) of the white sugar paste with the non-stick rolling pin so that it is large enough to cover the round drum board. Using the pastry brush, dampen the board with water and cover it with the rolled out sugar paste. Smooth and polish the surface with the cake smoother. Trim off the excess with the small sharp knife and set aside to dry for a couple of hours.

5 Using the large sharp knife, level the top of the cake then cut it in half horizontally. With the palette knife, spread one half with jam and the other half with buttercream, keeping a little aside to thinly coat the cake. Sandwich the two halves together and place upside down onto the spare board. Coat the top and sides of the cake with the remaining buttercream.

6 Roll out the remaining white sugar paste so that it is large enough to cover the top and sides of the cake. Cover and smooth the cake as shown on pages 8–9, taking care to retain the shape of the cake. Set aside to dry for about 2 hours then place in the centre of the covered drum board.

3

Piping the leaves onto the stems

7 With white royal icing and the No. 42 piping nozzle, pipe a shell around the base of the cake to hide the join. Now using the No. 2 nozzle and white royal icing, randomly pipe leaf stems over the top and sides of the cake. Once these have dried, use the No. 52 nozzle to pipe leaf shapes onto the stems. You will need to use a little pressure when piping the leaves (*see pic 3*).

8 While the leaves are still slightly soft, randomly attach the painted butterflies to the leaves. Use a little more royal icing if needed to secure the butterflies in place (*see pic 4*). Finally, decorate the edge of the drum board with lilac ribbon.

4

Attaching the butterflies to the cake

Masquerade

This cake will be a flamboyant theatrical centrepiece for any wedding day. The jewelled masks can be as highly decorated as your imagination allows.

YOU WILL NEED

- 30-cm (12-in) round fruit cake (see p 11)
- 25-cm (10-in) round fruit cake (see p 11)
- 21-cm (8-in) round fruit cake (see p 11)
- 5 kg (11 lb) white sugar paste (see p 13)
- Apricot glaze (see p 12)
- 5 kg (11 lb) marzipan
- 150 g (5½ oz) white royal icing (see p 12)
- Red and black food colouring
- 500 g (1 lb 2 oz) red coloured pastillage (see p 13)
- Gold scintillo or gold dust
- Isopropyl alcohol
- Icing (confectioner's) sugar in a sugar shaker

EQUIPMENT

- Large and small non-stick rolling pins
- 46-cm (18-in) round drum board
- Pastry brush
- Cake smoother
- Small sharp knife
- Large sharp knife
- 30-cm (12-in) round hard board
- 25-cm (10-in) round hard board
- 21-cm (8-in) round hard board
- 6 dowels
- Piping bags
- Nos. 1.5 and 5 piping nozzles
- Cellophane wrap
- 2½ m (98 in) red feather boa
- Non-stick board
- Craft knife
- Six party masks for moulds
- Sponge for drying
- 10 black feathers
- Bead maker
- Red ribbon to finish the drum board

1 Roll out approximately 225 g (8 oz) of the white sugar paste with the non-stick rolling pin so that it is large enough to cover the round drum board. Using the pastry brush, dampen the board with water and cover it with the rolled out sugar paste. Smooth and polish the surface with the cake smoother. Trim off the excess with the small sharp knife and set aside to dry for a couple of hours.

2 Using the large sharp knife, level the tops of all three cakes and turn them upside down onto hard boards of the same size. Brush the top and sides of the cakes with apricot glaze. Roll out the marzipan so that it is large enough to cover the top and sides of each cake. Cover and smooth all three cakes as shown on pages 8–9. Set aside to dry for about 12 hours.

3 Roll out the remaining white sugar paste, brush the marzipan with cooled boiled water and cover the top and sides of all three cakes with the sugar paste, using the method on page 9. Trim off the excess. Leave to dry for about 2 hours.

4 Dowel the bottom two tiers as shown on page 10. Stack the tiers one on top of the other using a little royal icing to stick each tier down. Using white royal icing and

1

Cutting out the mask template

2

Removing the dried mask from the party mask

the No. 5 piping nozzle, pipe a shell border around the bottom of each tier to hide the join. Wrap the red feather boa around the base of each tier, ensuring there is a piece of cellophane between the cake and the fur.

5 Photocopy the mask template on page 78 and cut it out. You will need 6 masks in total. Allow the coloured pastillage to rest for a few hours before using then, on the non-stick board, thinly roll out 85 g (3 oz) of it with the non-stick rolling pin. Place the template over the pastillage and cut around it with the craft knife (*see pic 1*). Carefully place the cut out shape on the inside of a party mask to dry into shape. Set aside to dry for 12 hours then gently remove it from the mould (*see pic 2*). Turn it onto a piece of sponge and allow to dry for a further 12 hours.

6 When the masks have dried, attach black feathers to the back of them with a little red royal icing. Using the bead maker, make a bead edging using the left over red pastillage used to make the masks (*see pic 3*) and attach to the top of each mask for a neat edge (*see pic 4*).

3

Making the beading

7 Using the No. 1.5 piping nozzle and black royal icing, decorate the bottom edges and eyes of the masks. The gold jewels are made with gold scintillo mixed with a few drops of isopropyl alcohol. Using a No. 1.5 nozzle pipe jewelled decorations around the eye openings and the borders of each mask (*see pic 5*). You can use royal icing for the jewelled ornaments instead, painting them with gold dust mixed with a few drops of isopropyl alcohol when dry. Place the masks on to the cake, as shown in the final picture. To help the top mask stand in place, put a small ball of white sugar paste on to the cake to support it from behind then hide the support with some red feathers. Finally, decorate the edge of the drum board with red ribbon.

Note: As the masks are for decoration purposes only, they can be decorated with non-edible decorations.

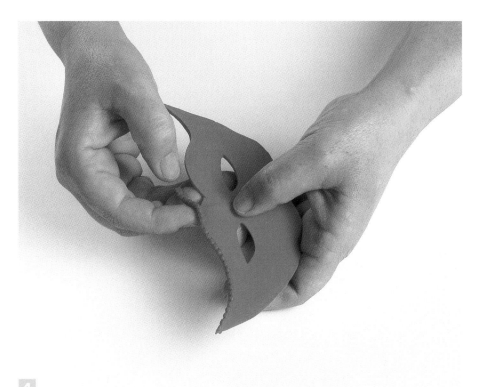

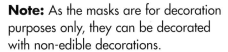

Attaching the bead edging to the top of the mask

Piping the gold jewels

Night and day

This modern two-tier cake with its edible suns and moons makes an ideal cake for a teenage birthday celebration.

YOU WILL NEED

- 21-cm (8-in) round fruit cake (see p 11)
- 15-cm (6-in) round fruit cake (see p 11)
- 2 kg (4 lb 6 oz) dark blue sugar paste (see p 13)
- Apricot glaze (see p 12)
- 2 kg (4 lb 6 oz) marzipan
- Gold and silver dragees
- 150 g (5½ oz) flower paste (see p 13)
- 100 g (3½ oz) white royal icing (see p 12)
- Gold and silver dusts
- Isopropyl alcohol
- Icing (confectioner's) sugar in a sugar shaker

EQUIPMENT

- Large and small non-stick rolling pins
- 30-cm (12-in) round drum board
- Pastry brush
- Cake smoother
- Small sharp knife
- Large sharp knife
- 21cm (8-in) round hard board
- 15-cm (6-in) round hard board
- 3 dowels
- Piping bags
- Nos. 1.5 and 2 piping nozzles
- Fine paintbrush
- Tweezers

- Non-stick board
- Sunflower cutter
- Round cutter
- Small star cutter
- Sponge for drying
- No. 1.5 piping nozzle
- 2 food-grade flower picks
- 15 gold and silver wires
- Gold ribbon to finish the drum board

1 Roll out approximately 150 g (5½ oz) of the dark blue sugar paste with the non-stick rolling pin so that it is large enough to cover the round drum board. Using the pastry brush, dampen the board with water and cover it with the rolled out sugar paste. Smooth and polish the surface with the cake smoother. Trim off the excess with the small sharp knife and set aside to dry for a couple of hours.

2 Using the large sharp knife, level the top of both cakes and turn them upside down onto hard boards of the same size. Brush the top and sides with apricot glaze. Roll out the marzipan so that it is large enough to cover the top and sides of each cake. Cover and smooth the cakes as shown on pages 8–9. Set aside to dry for about 12 hours.

3 Roll out the remaining dark blue sugar paste, brush the marzipan with cooled boiled water and cover the top and sides of both cakes with the sugar paste, using the method on page 9. Trim off the excess and keep a walnut-size piece to one side for piping. Leave to dry for about 2 hours then place the bottom cake in the centre of the covered drum board. Dowel the bottom tier as shown on page 10.

4 Soften the walnut-size piece of sugar paste with a little water to a piping consistency. Using the No. 2 piping nozzle, pipe a shell border around the base of the lower tier to hide the join (see pic 1). You will need to repeat this process with the top tier.

Piping a shell to hide the join

5 While the covering is still soft, randomly push in gold and silver dragees over the two cakes. You will need to dot the surface using the paintbrush dipped in a little water before pushing in the dragees to ensure good adhesion. You may find it easier to use tweezers to handle the dragees (see pic 2).

6 Place the top tier centrally onto the bottom tier using a little royal icing to stick the tiers together. Repeat Step 4 to pipe the border.

Inserting the dragees

7 Thinly roll out the flower paste on the non-stick board and cut out three suns using the sunflower cutter. Next, cut out three moons using the round cutter then cut into the circle again to form a crescent (see pic 3). Finally, stamp out approximately 15 to 20 stars. Leave the shapes to dry on a piece of sponge (see pic 4).

8 Using the No. 1.5 piping nozzle, pipe faces onto the suns and moons with white royal icing. When dry, paint the suns gold, the moons silver and the stars a mixture of both colours using gold and silver dusts mixed with a few drop of isopropyl alcohol (see pic 5). Attach the embellishments to the cake with royal icing. Insert the gold and silver wires into food-grade flower picks and secure them into the bottom tier. Finally, decorate the edge of the drum board with gold ribbon.

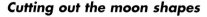

Cutting out the moon shapes

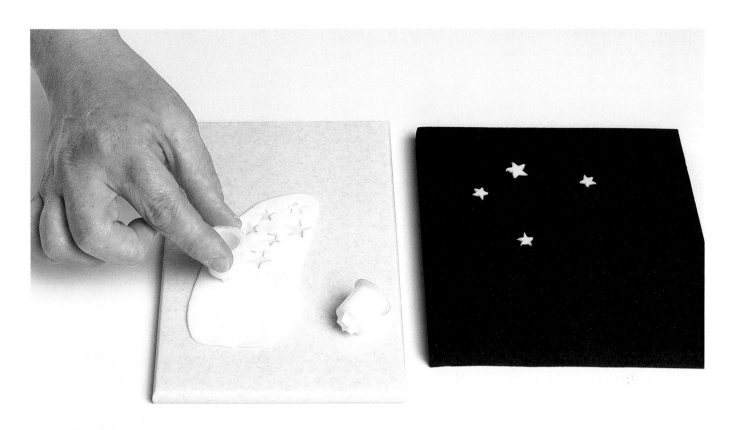

4

Stamping out the stars

5

Painting the suns, moons and stars

Oasis in the desert

The jewelled colours on this cake are inspired by the Arabian Nights tales. The bright colours contrast well with the yellow covering.

YOU WILL NEED

- 21-cm (8-in) square fruit cake (see p 11)
- 1 kg (2 lb 3 oz) yellow sugar paste (see p 13)
- Apricot glaze (see p 12)
- 1 kg (2 lb 3 oz) marzipan
- Yellow and green food colouring
- 100 g (3½ oz) royal icing coloured yellow (see p 12)
- 100 g (3½ oz) castor sugar coloured yellow (see p 13)
- 100 g (3½ oz) each of black, green, pink, orange, blue and purple sugar paste (see p 13)
- 120 g (4½ oz) brown sugar paste (see p 13)
- Sugar glue (see p 12)
- 75 g (2½ oz) flower paste coloured green (see p 13)
- Icing (confectioner's) sugar in a sugar shaker

EQUIPMENT

- Large and small non-stick rolling pins
- 28-cm (11-in) square drum board
- Pastry brush
- Cake smoother
- Small sharp knife
- Large sharp knife
- Spare board
- Piping bags
- No. 1.5 piping nozzle
- Patterned strip cutter
- Craft knife
- Ten 24-g white wires
- Green florist tape
- Yellow ribbon to finish the drum board

1 Roll out approximately 150 g (5½ oz) of the yellow sugar paste with the non-stick rolling pin so that it is large enough to cover the square drum board. Using the pastry brush, dampen the board with water and cover it with the rolled out sugar paste. Smooth and polish the surface with the cake smoother. Trim off the excess with the small sharp knife and set aside to dry for a couple of hours.

2 Using the large sharp knife, level the top of the cake, turn it upside down and place it on the spare board. Brush the top and sides with apricot glaze. Roll out the marzipan so that it is large enough to cover the top and sides of the cake. Cover and smooth the cake as shown on pages 8–9. Set aside to dry for about 2 hours.

3 Set aside 100 g (3½ oz) of yellow sugar paste for Step 5. Roll out the remaining yellow sugar paste, brush the marzipan with cooled boiled water and cover the top and sides of the cake with the sugar paste using the method on page 9. Trim off the excess and keep a walnut-size piece to one side for piping. Leave to dry for about 2 hours then place the cake in the centre of the covered drum board.

4 Soften the walnut-size piece of sugar paste with a little water to a piping consistency. Using the

No. 1.5 piping nozzle, pipe a shell border around the base of the cake to hide the join and smooth over with your finger. Brush a thin coat of watered-down yellow royal icing around the base of the board and while damp, sprinkle with the yellow caster sugar.

5 Roll out the black sugar paste and cut four 13 x 5-cm (5¼ x 2-in) rectangles. Stick these centrally onto each side of the cake with a little royal icing. To make the pelmet, roll out the blue sugar paste and cut two 8 x 4-cm (3¼ x 1¾-in) rectangles. Pinch both ends to create folds and stick down with a little royal icing so that they overlap the top of the black rectangle. To make the inner curtains, roll out the blue sugar paste and cut

two 7 x 5-cm (3 x 2-in) rectangles. Create pleats as shown in the picture and stick down with a little royal icing at either side of the black rectangle (*see pic 1*). Repeat with the green and pink sugar pastes and the reserved yellow sugar paste from Step 3. Attach the curtains to the other three sides of the cake.

6 To make the stripy outer curtains, roll out the purple sugar paste and cut two 7 x 5-cm (3 x 2-in) rectangles. Cut thin stripes of pink sugar paste and arrange them over the purple rectangles. Use the small non-stick rolling pin to embed the stripes into the purple sugar paste. Create pleats as in the previous step and stick them to each corner of the cake using a little royal icing, making sure they slightly overlap

the inner curtains (*see pic 2*). Repeat for the other three sets of stripy curtains, using two colours for each set. To make the decorative border, roll out a small amount of coloured sugar paste into a strip the length of the cake and use the patterned strip cutter to cut out the shape. Stick it down with a little royal icing.

Attaching the outer curtains

7 Roll out a piece of blue sugar paste and with the craft knife cut out a shape that resembles a small lake. Attach it to the top of the cake with a little water. To make the tree trunk, roll 15 g (½ oz) of brown sugar paste into a ball and then flatten it so that it resembles a small disc. Repeat the proccess so that you have a total of 8 discs, making sure each disc is slightly smaller than the previous. Stack the discs on top of one another, with the largest one at the bottom, and glue them together with sugar glue (*see pic 3*).

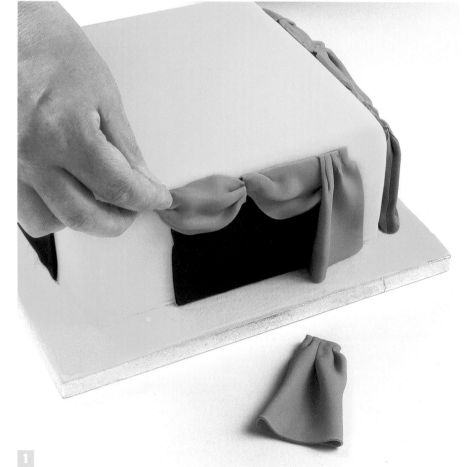

Attaching the pelmet and the inner curtains

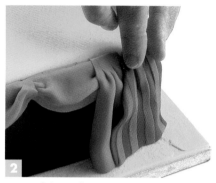

Making the tree trunk

4

Making the palm leaves

8 To make the palm leaves, roll a small amount of the green flower paste into a ball then into a sausage shape. Dip the wire in sugar glue and push it into the sausage shape. Flatten the shape with the small non-stick rolling pin and with the craft knife, cut out a leaf shape then set aside to dry and harden for a couple of hours. Repeat the process 9 more times. When all the leaves are hard, tape the wires together at the base of the leaves with florist tape, arranging the leaves to form the top of the palm tree. Cut any excess wire leaving 2½ cm (1 in) to insert into the trunk (*see pic 4*).

9 Attach the base of the trunk to the top of the cake with a dab of royal icing then push the taped together leaves into the top of the trunk (*see pic 5*). Finally, decorate the edge of the drum board with the ribbon.

5

Assembling the tree

Farmyard wedding

This three-tier cake is a wedding cake with a difference! All the animals are dressed up in their Sunday best for the big day!

YOU WILL NEED

- 28-cm (11-in) round fruit cake (see p 11)
- 21-cm (8-in) round fruit cake (see p 11)
- 15-cm (6-in) round fruit cake (see p 11)
- 5¾ kg (12 lb 11 oz) white sugar paste (see p 13)
- Apricot glaze (see p 12)
- 6½ kg (14 lb 5 oz) marzipan
- Blue, green, black, brown, yellow, and pink food colouring
- Isopropyl alcohol
- 150 g (5½ oz) white royal icing (see p 12)
- 100 g (3½ oz) pale blue coloured royal icing (see p 12)

- 75 g (2½ oz) brown coloured royal icing (see p 12)
- Icing (confectioner's) sugar in a sugar shaker

EQUIPMENT

- Large and small non-stick rolling pins
- 36-cm (14-in) round drum board
- Pastry brush
- Cake smoother
- Small sharp knife
- Large sharp knife
- 28-cm (11-in) round hard board
- 21-cm (8-in) round hard board

- 15-cm (6-in) round hard board
- 6 dowels
- Natural sponge for sponging
- Thin rubber gloves
- Stiff paintbrush
- 5 strands of dried spaghetti
- Metal sieve
- Craft knife
- Cocktail sticks
- Fine paintbrush
- Sugarcraft gun fitted with a perforated disc
- Pale blue ribbon to finish the drum board

1 Roll out approximately 175 g (6 oz) of the white sugar paste with the non-stick rolling pin so that it is large enough to cover the round drum board. Using the pastry brush, dampen the board with water and cover it with the rolled out sugar paste. Smooth and polish the surface with the cake smoother. Trim off the excess with the small sharp knife and set aside to dry for a couple of hours.

2 Using the large sharp knife, level the tops of all three cakes and turn them upside down onto hard boards of the same size. Brush the top and sides of the cakes with apricot glaze. Set aside 1½ kg (3 lb 5 oz) of marzipan to make the animals. Roll out the remaining marzipan so that it is large enough to cover the top and sides of each cake. Cover and smooth all three cakes as shown on pages 8–9. Set aside to dry for about 12 hours.

3 Set aside 750 g (1 lb 10 oz) of white sugarpaste to make the accessories and the animals. Roll out the remaining white sugar paste, brush the marzipan with cooled boiled water and cover the top and sides of all three cakes with the sugar paste, using the method on page 9. Trim off the excess. Leave to dry for about 12 hours then dowel the bottom two tiers as shown on page 10.

Sponging the cake

4 Sponge each tier to create sky and grass effects using blue and green food colouring made into a wash with a few drops of isopropyl alcohol (*see pic 1*). Sponge the surface of the top tier green. Wear rubber gloves to do this to avoid staining your hands. When dry, stack the tiers one on top of the other using a little royal icing to stick each tier down.

5 Using the pale blue royal icing softened with a little water, stipple the drum board using a stiff paintbrush to create a water effect. Make the rocks by colouring 100 g (3½ oz) of left-over sugar paste grey using black food colouring. Undermixing the paste will achieve a marbly, more natural texture to the rocks. Attach them to the drum board with dabs of royal icing. To make the reeds, break the spaghetti into twelve 5-cm (2-in) pieces. Hold them over a boiling kettle and gently bend the tip. Roll a small amount of brown sugar paste into a sausage shape and attach it to the spaghetti with sugar glue, teasing it to a point. Insert the reeds in the gaps of the rocks with dabs of royal icing (*see pic 2*).

6 Moving on to the top of the lower tier, stipple brown royal icing on the edges to create a muddy effect. Add yellow strands of sugar paste to brown royal icing to make the straw.

7 Make the gate that will rest on the side of the top tier with brown sugar paste and attach it with a little water. Using green sugar paste softened with a little water, push the sugar paste through the metal sieve with the back of a spoon to create the grass (*see pic 3*). Carefully scrape it off with the craft knife and attach it around the base of the top tier and around the rocks on the drum board, using a little water to stick it down.

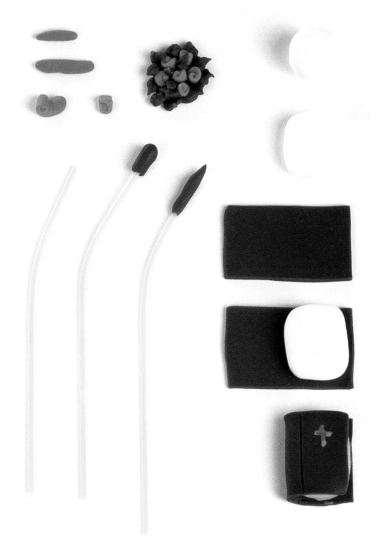

Making the accessories

Making the grass

8 Use the marzipan set aside from Step 2 to make the animals. If the marzipan is too soft, add a little icing sugar to help stiffen it. Make sure you work the paste until it is smooth and free of cracks. When colouring the

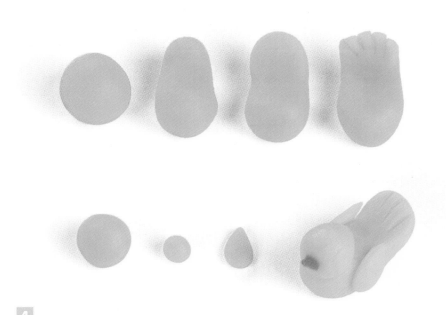

4

Making the ducks

paste, thoroughly work in the colour to ensure there is no colour spotting. When modelling with marzipan it is important to keep all your equipment clean. Use a little water to attach the pieces of marzipan together and strands of spaghetti to join heads to bodies, as shown in the photograph.

To make the ducks
This quantity makes 10 ducks
◆ 400 g (14 oz) yellow-coloured marzipan divided into the following quantities:
• Body: 20 g (¾ oz)
• Head: 15 g (½ oz)
• Wings: 5 g (¼ oz)
Roll the body into a ball, removing any cracks, then model into a pear shape. Pinch the narrow end and mark it with a cocktail stick for tail feathers. Gently flatten the base to form the body. Model the head with a beak and mark in the eyes with the cocktail stick. To make the wings, roll two small balls from the wings quantity and model each into tear shapes. Mark them for wings with the cocktail stick and stick them to the sides of the body (*see pic 4*).

To make the pigs
This quantity makes eight pigs
◆ 480 g (1 lb 1 oz) pink marzipan divided into the following quantities:
• Body: 30 g (1 oz)
• Head: 15 g (½ oz)
• Legs: 5 g (¼ oz)

• Tail: 5 g (¼ oz)
• Ears: 5 g (¼ oz)
Roll the body into a ball, removing any cracks, then model into a peanut shape. Model the head with a snout and mark in the nose and mouth with the cocktail stick. For the back legs, roll the marzipan into a ball and then a sausage shape 2½ cm (1 in) long. Mark the toes as in the picture and stick on either side of the body. To make the arms, roll the marzipan into a ball and then a sausage shape 3½ cm (1½ in) long. Mark the hands and toes and stick into place. Support the head by inserting a small piece of spaghetti into the top of the body and place the head on top of it, securing it with a little water. To make the tail, make a thin roll, twist it then stick it to the body. Roll the marzipan into a ball then a pear shape and flatten to make the ears. Mark the inside with the cocktail stick and attach it to the head. Repeat for the other ear. Finally, using a fine paintbrush, paint in the eyes with black food colouring (*see pic 5*).

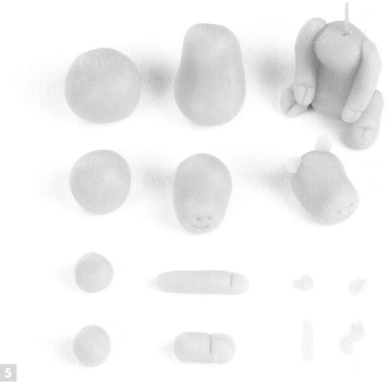

5

Making the pigs

7

Making the sheeps' coat

6

Making the sheep

To make the sheep
This quantity makes six sheep
◆ 300 g (10½ oz) white sugar paste
◆ 400 g (14 oz) black marzipan
  divided into the following quantities:
• Body: 30 g (1 oz)
• Head: 15 g (½ oz)
• Arms: 10 g (⅓ oz)
• Legs: 10 g (⅓ oz)
• Ears: 2 g (⅛ oz)

To make the body, roll the marzipan into a ball and then a pear shape. Stand on the fat end. To make the legs, make two sausage shapes 2½ cm (1 in) long and mark the toes with the cocktail stick as shown. Secure them to the body. Roll two sausage shapes 4 cm (2½ in) in length to make the arms and mark as for the toes and secure on either side of the body. For the ears, roll the marzipan into a ball then a pear shape and flatten. Mark inside with the cocktail stick and attach it to the head. Repeat for the other ear (*see pic 6*). Make the sheeps' coat with softened white sugar paste in the sugarcraft gun fitted with a perforated disc. Dampen the body with a little water and carefully stick the strands of sugar paste to the body (*see pic 7*).

To make the cows
This quantity makes three cows
◆ 310 g (11 oz) white sugar paste
◆ 70 g (2½ oz) black sugar paste
◆ Sugar glue
Divide the white sugar paste into the following quantities:
• Body: 50 g (2 oz)
• Legs: 10 g (⅓ oz)
• Arms: 10 g (⅓ oz)
• Head: 25 g (1 oz)
• Ears: 2 g (⅛ oz)
• Tail: 5 g (¼ oz)

To make the body, roll the sugar paste into a ball then a pear shape. Stand on the fat end. To make the legs, make two sausage shapes 3½ cm (1½ in) long. Roll two black sugar paste balls and attach them to the end of each leg with sugar glue. Repeat with the arms and attach as shown in the picture. To make the head, roll the sugar paste into a ball then a peanut shape. Attach the head to the body. Cut a small circle of black sugar paste and attach it to the front of the head. Mark the mouth and nostrils with the cocktail stick. To make the ears, roll the sugar paste into a ball then a pear shape and flatten. Mark the inside of the ears and place them on the head. To make the tail, roll the sugar paste into a long sausage shape and attach to the back. Shape the black sugar paste into flat, uneven shapes and stick randomly on the body (*see pic 8*).

Place all the animal models onto cake as shown.

8

Making the cows

Simply black and white

This cake has clean-cut lines that are accentuated with the simple colour scheme.

YOU WILL NEED

- 1½ kg (3 lb 5 oz) black sugar paste (see p 13)
- 1½ kg (3 lb 5 oz) white sugar paste (see p 13)
- 25-cm (10-in) round fruit cake (see p 11)
- Two 15-cm (6-in) teardrop-shaped fruit cakes (use 8-in round mixture between two cakes, see p 11)
- Apricot glaze (see p 12)
- 3 kg (6 lb 10 oz) marzipan
- 50 g (2 oz) royal icing (see p 12)
- Icing (confectioner's) sugar in a sugar shaker

EQUIPMENT

- 36-cm (14-in) round drum board
- Sheet of greaseproof paper
- Pencil
- Scissors
- Pastry brush
- Large non-stick rolling pin
- Ruler

- Small sharp knife
- Cake smoother
- Small sharp knife
- Large sharp knife
- Spare board
- Two 15-cm (6-in) teardrop-shaped hard boards
- 8-cm (3-in) round cutter
- Black and white ribbon to finish the cakes and the drum board

1 Place the drum board on the sheet of greaseproof paper and pencil around the outline. Cut out the circle then fold it in half. Using the pastry brush, dampen one half of the board with water. Roll out approximately 150 g (5½ oz) of the black sugar paste with the non-stick rolling pin so that it is large enough to cover half the

1
Covering the drum board

board. Using the ruler and the small sharp knife, cut a straight line (making sure it is slightly longer than the diameter of the board). Next, place the folded circle template on the dry half of the board and the black sugar paste on the damp half, taking care to line up the straight edge of the sugar paste with the straight edge of the template. Smooth and polish the surface with the cake smoother. Trim off the excess with the the small sharp knife (*see pic 1*). Repeat the process with the white sugar paste, making sure to butt the white against the black. Set aside to dry for a couple of hours.

2 Using the large sharp knife, level the tops of all three cakes and turn them upside down. Place the round cake onto the spare board and the teardrop-shaped cakes onto hard boards of the same size. Brush the top

and sides of the cakes with apricot glaze. Roll out 2 kg (4 lb 7 oz) of the marzipan so that it is large enough to cover the top and sides of the round cake. Cover and smooth the cake as shown on pages 8–9. Set aside to dry for about 2 hours. With the remaining marzipan, cover both teardrop-shaped cakes in the same way.

3 Make another greaseproof paper circle the size of the base cake (25 cm/10 in) and fold it in half. Roll out 1 kg (2 lb 3 oz) of the black sugar paste so that it is large enough to cover the top and sides of half the cake. Using the ruler and the small sharp knife, cut a straight line (making sure it is slightly longer than the top and sides of the cake). Brush the marzipan with cooled boiled water and place the folded circle template on the dry half of the cake and the black sugar paste on the damp half, taking

2

Covering the cake

care to line up the straight edge of the sugar paste with the straight edge of the template. Smooth and polish the surface with the cake smoother. Trim off the excess. Repeat the process with the white sugar paste, making sure to keep the join between the two colours straight (*see pic 2*). Leave to dry for about 2 hours then place the cake in the centre of the covered drum board, making sure the cake and board colours are opposing.

4 Cover one teardrop cake with the remaining black sugar paste and the other with white sugar paste, using the same method as above. Set aside to dry for about 2 hours. Decorate each side of the round cake and each teardrop with ribbon the same colour as the sugar paste (*see pic 3*). When dry, place each teardrop on opposing coloured sides of the base cake using a little royal icing to stick them down (*see pic 4*).

5 Stamp out two 7-cm (3-in) sugar paste circles, one black one white, and cut each circle in half. Place one half of each circle onto the opposing sides of the base cake where the join meets, as seen in final image. Finally, Decorate the edge of the drum board with black ribbon.

3

Decorating the cake with ribbon

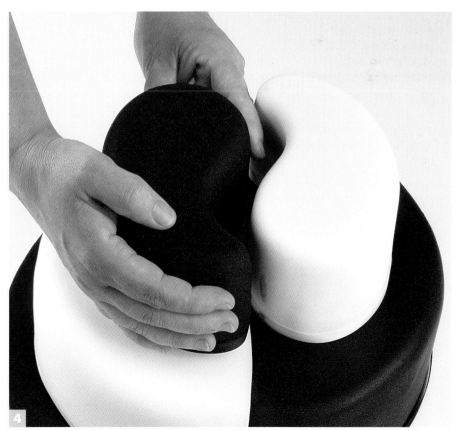

4

Positioning the teardrop-shaped cakes

A *star is born*

This delicate cake is perfect to celebrate the birth of a baby or even for a christening. The colours can be changed to pink for a girl.

YOU WILL NEED

- 25-cm (10-in) square fruit cake (see p 11)
- Apricot glaze (see p 12)
- 800 g (1 lb 12 oz) marzipan
- 100 g (3½ oz) white sugar paste (see p 13)
- 1 kg (2 lb 3 oz) pale blue sugar paste (see p 13)
- 150 g (5½ oz) white royal icing (see p 12)
- Silver dust
- Isopropyl alcohol
- 25 g (1 oz) flesh-coloured sugar paste (see p 13)
- 25 g (1 oz) dark blue sugar paste (see p 13)
- Dark blue food colouring
- Icing (confectioner's) sugar in a sugar shaker

EQUIPMENT

- Sheet of greaseproof paper
- Scissors
- Large sharp knife
- Spare board
- Pastry brush
- Large and small non-stick rolling pins
- Cake smoother
- 5-cm (2-in) round cutter
- Small star cutter
- Craft knife
- Sponge for drying
- Small sharp knife
- 36-cm (14-in) round drum board
- Palette knife
- Fine paintbrush
- Piping bag
- No. 1.5 piping nozzle
- White ribbon to finish the drum board

1 Trace the star template on page 79 onto a sheet of greaseproof paper and cut it out. Using the large sharp knife, level the top of the cake, turn it upside down and place it on the spare board. Place the star template over the cake and cut around the template so that you get a star shape (*see pic 1*). Brush the top and sides with apricot glaze. Roll out the marzipan so that it is large enough to cover the top and sides of the cake. Cover and smooth the cake as shown on pages 8–9, taking care with the points of the star. Set aside to dry for about 2 hours.

Carving out the cake

2 Roll out the white sugar paste, reserving 25 g (1 oz) for the crib. Stamp out the moon using the round cutter then cut into the circle again to form a crescent. Next stamp out approximately 15 stars and cut out 10 cloud shapes with the craft knife. Leave the shapes to dry on a piece of sponge.

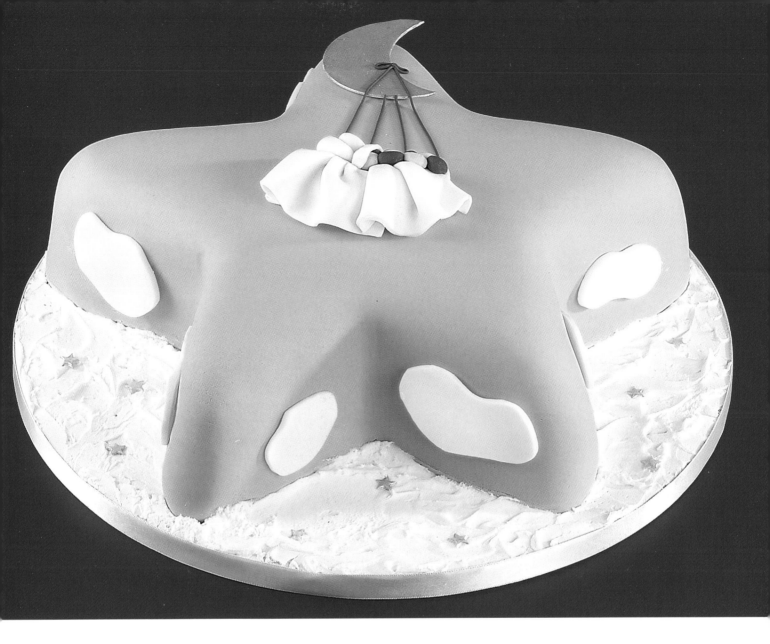

3 Set aside 50 g (2 oz) of pale blue sugar paste for the crib. Roll out the remaining sugar paste, brush the marzipan with cooled boiled water and cover the top and sides of the cake with the sugar paste, using the method on page 9. Trim off the excess with the small sharp knife. Leave to dry for about 2 hours then place the cake in the centre of the drum board.

4 Set aside a small amount of white royal icing for the string of the crib. Thinly spread the remainder onto the drum board and roughen slightly with the palette knife to give a cloud effect (see pic 2). When the moon and stars have hardened, paint them

Covering the board with royal icing

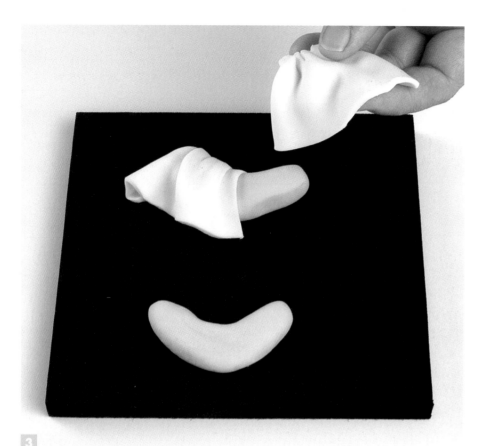

3

Assembling the base of the crib

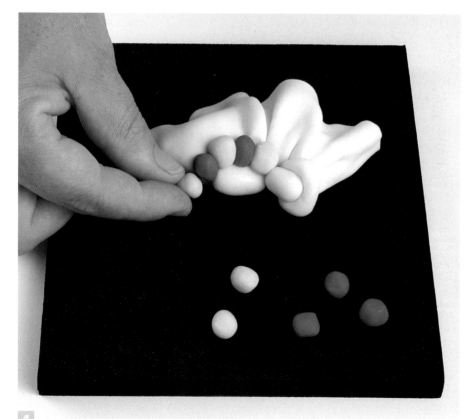

4

Making the quilt to cover the baby

with silver dust mixed with a few drops of isopropyl alcohol. Stick the moon down with a dab of royal icing at the tip of one of the cake's points. Stick the stars randomly on the textured drum board. Finally, stick down one cloud per side with a little royal icing.

5 To make the crib, make a 5-cm (2-in) banana shape out of the pale blue sugar paste set aside from Step 3. Roll out most of the white sugar paste set aside from Step 2 into a 7 x 2½-cm (3 x 1-in) rectangle. Pleat it so that it looks like material then place it over the banana shape to make the base of the crib (see pic 3). Roll another small piece of white sugar paste into an oblong pillow to fit the size of the crib. Model two-thirds of the flesh-coloured sugar paste into an oval for the baby's body and place it in the crib. Make a smaller oval with the remaining paste and place it on top of the pillow. Using the dark blue sugar paste and the remaining white sugar paste, alternate small balls to make the quilt to cover the baby (see pic 4). Using a scrap of white sugar paste, add a small strip to the top of the quilt to finish it off.

6 Colour the remaining white royal icing dark blue and, using the No. 1.5 piping nozzle, pipe strings from the crib over the hook of the moon finishing with a bow (see pic 5). Finally, decorate the edge of the drum board with white ribbon.

5

Piping the strings

Shades of the Orient

The inspiration for this cake comes from the patterns on Japanese kimonos. The rich colours and gold leaves are familiar features of Japanese design.

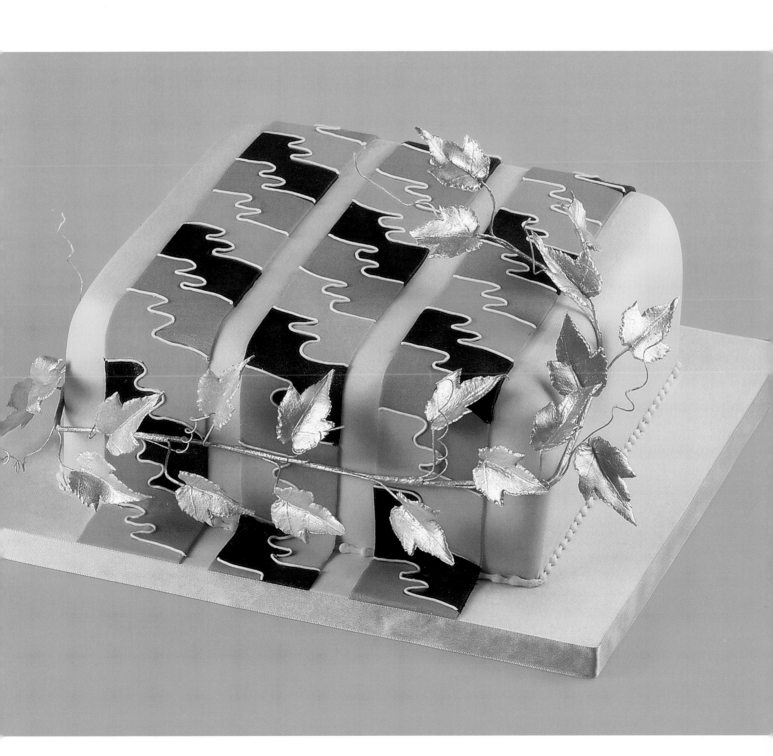

YOU WILL NEED

- Cream and autumn leaf food colouring
- 1.1 kg (2 lb 7 oz) mustard-coloured sugar paste (see p 13)
- 21-cm (8-in) square fruit cake (see p 11)
- Apricot glaze (see p 12)
- 1.1 kg (2 lb 7 oz) marzipan
- 250 g (9 oz) each of red, orange and black sugar paste (see p 13)
- Gum tragacanth
- 50 g (2 oz) royal icing coloured dark yellow (see p 12)
- 50 g (2 oz) flower paste (see p 13)

- Sugar glue (see p 12)
- Gold dust
- Icing (confectioner's) sugar in a sugar shaker

EQUIPMENT

- Large and small non-stick rolling pins
- 30-cm (12-in) square drum board
- Pastry brush
- Cake smoother
- Small sharp knife
- Large sharp knife
- Spare board

- Piping bags
- Nos. 1 and 1.5 piping nozzles
- Scissors
- Craft knife
- Ivy leaf cutter
- 25 half length 26-g white wires
- Ivy leaf veiner
- Softening pad
- Ball tool
- Sponge for drying
- White florist tape
- Mustard ribbon to finish the drum board

1 If you cannot get hold of mustard-coloured sugar paste, you can mix the colour yourself by colouring white sugar paste with a mix of cream and autumn leaf food colouring. Once you have achieved the right colour, set it aside to rest for a couple of hours before using.

2 Roll out approximately 150 g (5½ oz) of the mustard sugar paste with the non-stick rolling pin so that it is large enough to cover the square drum board. Using the pastry brush, dampen the board with water and cover it with the rolled out sugar paste. Smooth and polish the surface with the cake smoother. Trim off the excess with the small sharp knife and set aside to dry for a couple of hours.

3 Using the large sharp knife, level the top of the cake, turn it upside down and place it on the spare board. Brush the top and sides with apricot glaze. Roll out the marzipan so that it is large enough to cover the top and sides of the cake. Cover and smooth the cake as shown on pages 8–9. Set aside to dry for about 2 hours.

4 Roll out the remaining mustard sugar paste, brush the marzipan with cooled boiled water and cover the top and sides of the cake with the sugar paste, using the method on page 9. Trim off the excess and keep a walnut-size piece to one side for piping. Leave to dry for about 2 hours then place the cake in the centre of the drum board.

5 Soften the walnut-size piece of sugar paste with a little water to a piping consistency. Using the No. 1.5 piping nozzle, pipe a shell border around the base of the cake to hide the join.

6 Photocopy the template on page 79. Cut out the shape and place it on the thinly rolled out red, orange and black sugar pastes mixed with half a teaspoon of gum tragacanth for each colour. Cut around the shape with the craft knife and stick the pieces on the top of the cake with a little water. Make sure you alternate the colours and that you do not distort the shapes when moving them. With the No. 1 piping nozzle and dark yellow royal icing, pipe a line following the joins in the pattern (see pic 1).

Decorating the top of the cake

Stamping out the ivy leaves

7 To make the ivy leaves, roll out the flower paste leaving a ridge in the middle of the paste for the wire to be pushed into. Stamp out 20 to 25 leaves with the ivy leaf cutter (*see pic 2*). Dip the end of the wire into the sugar glue then push it into the paste at the ridged end. Work the wire half way up the leaf and vein it with ivy leaf veiner (*see pic 3*).

Inserting wire into the ridge

8 Soften the leaf on a softening pad with the ball tool to achieve thin edges and to give the leaf movement then leave to dry on a piece of sponge. When dry, dust with gold dust and steam over a kettle to seal the colour (*see pic 4*). Repeat for the other leaves.

Sealing the colour

9 Tape the leaves together with white florist tape to make a branch of ivy, dusting the taped wire with gold dust. Place onto the cake to finish off. Finally, decorate the edge of the drum board with mustard ribbon.

Daisy, daisy

Clean lines of yellow and white give this cake a fresh look for summer. Daisies complement this cake and are very popular with young brides.

YOU WILL NEED

- 25-cm (10-in) square fruit cake (see p 11)
- 15-cm (6-in) square fruit cake (see p 11)
- 3 kg (6 lb 10 oz) white sugar paste (see p 13)
- Apricot glaze (see p 12)
- 3 kg (6 lb 10 oz) marzipan
- 2 kg (4 lb 6 oz) yellow sugar paste (see p 13)
- 100 g (3½ oz) flower paste (see p 13)
- 100 g (3½ oz) royal icing (see p 12)
- 50 g (2 oz) pale green sugar paste (see p 13)
- Icing (confectioner's) sugar in a sugar shaker

EQUIPMENT

- Large and small non-stick rolling pins
- 36-cm (14-in) square drum board
- Pastry brush
- Cake smoother
- Small sharp knife
- Large sharp knife
- Spare board
- 15-cm (6-in) square hard board
- 3 dowels
- Ribbon cutter
- Craft knife
- Piping bags
- No. 2 piping nozzle
- Non-stick board
- Daisy cutter
- Sponge for drying
- 2½-cm (1-in) round cutter
- White ribbon to finish the drum board

1 Roll out approximately 175 g (6 oz) of the white sugar paste with the non-stick rolling pin so that it is large enough to cover the square drum board. Using the pastry brush, dampen the board with water and cover it with the rolled out sugar paste. Smooth and polish the surface with the cake smoother. Trim off the excess with the small sharp knife and set aside to dry for a couple of hours.

2 Using the large sharp knife, level the top of each cake, turn them upside down and place the larger cake onto the spare board and the smaller one onto a hard board of the same size. Brush the top and sides of the cakes with apricot glaze. Roll out the marzipan so that it is large enough to cover the top and sides of each cake. Cover and smooth the cakes as shown on pages 8–9. Set aside to dry for about 12 hours.

3 Roll out the remaining white sugar paste, brush the marzipan with cooled boiled water and cover the top and sides of both cakes with the sugar paste, using the method on page 9. Leave to dry for about 2 hours then place the bottom cake in the centre of the covered drum board. Dowel the bottom tier as shown on page 10.

4 Roll out the yellow sugar paste. Using the ribbon cutter with a 2½-cm (1-in) gap, cut a strip of yellow sugar paste long enough to go over the top and sides of the larger cake. Stick each strip down with a little water, working from the centre of the cake outwards and leaving a 2½-cm (1-in) space between each strip. Trim the ends of each strip a little short to leave enough space to pipe a border around the base of the cake (*see pic 1*).

5 When all the strips in one direction are in place, place a second set of strips perpendicularly over the top, again working from the centre outwards. Carefully cut away the overlapping pieces with the craft knife (*see pic 2*). Remember to trim the ends of each strip a little short to leave enough space to pipe a border around the base of the cake.

6 Repeat the above two steps for the smaller cake then place it on top of the bottom cake, using a little royal icing to stick it down. With white royal icing and the No. 2 piping nozzle, pipe a small shell around the base of each tier to hide the join (*see pic 3*).

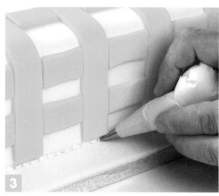

Piping a shell to hide the join

7 To make the daisies, thinly roll out the flower paste on the non-stick board and stamp out 12 daisy shapes. Place them on a mould to dry until hard, lightly turning up the petals to give a sense of three-dimension (*see pic 4*). When dry, stick two daisies together with a little royal icing, positioning them so that the bottom petals and top petals alternate.

Sticking the strips down

Removing the overlapping squares of sugarpaste

4

Making the daisies and leaves

5

Attaching the daisies with royal icing

8 With the remaining yellow sugar paste, cut out seven 2½-cm (1-in) circles and mark with the tip of a piping nozzle to give a daisy centre effect. When dry, stick a circle in the centre of each daisy with a dab of royal icing. Cut out nine leaf shapes from the pale green sugar paste and leave to dry on a piece of sponge.

9 When the daisies and leaves are dry, stick them in place as shown in the final picture with a little royal icing (*see pic 5*). Note that the top of the cake has three daisies resting against each other. Finally, decorate the edge of the drum board with white ribbon.

Fruit frenzy

The opulence of the fruit on this cake together with the simplicity of the covering perfectly balance this design.

YOU WILL NEED

- 25-cm (10-in) round fruit cake (see p 11)
- 15-cm (6-in) round fruit cake (see p 11)
- 3 kg (6 lb 10 oz) white sugar paste (see p 13)
- Apricot glaze (see p 12)
- 5½ kg (12 lb 2 oz) marzipan
- 100 g (3½ oz) royal icing (see p 12)
- Green, brown, orange, red, yellow, dark red and blue food colouring
- Red dust
- Sugar glue (see p 12)
- Icing (confectioner's) sugar in a sugar shaker

EQUIPMENT

- Large non-stick rolling pin
- 46-cm (18-in) round drum board
- Pastry brush
- Cake smoother
- Small sharp knife
- Large sharp knife
- 25-cm (10-in) round hard board
- 15-cm (6-in) round hard board
- 3 dowels
- Piping bags
- No. 5 piping nozzle
- Star tool
- Grater
- Calyx cutter
- Cocktail sticks
- White ribbon to finish the drum board

1 Roll out approximately 225 g (8 oz) of the white sugar paste with the non-stick rolling pin so that it is large enough to cover the round drum board. Using the pastry brush, dampen the board with water and cover it with the rolled out sugar paste. Smooth and polish the surface with the cake smoother. Trim off the excess with the small sharp knife and set aside to dry for a couple of hours.

2 Using the large sharp knife, level the top of each cake, carve out a quarter section from each cake (*see pic 1*) and turn them upside down onto hard boards of the same size with a quarter wedge also cut out of them. Brush the top and sides of the cakes with apricot glaze. Set aside 2½ kg (5 lb 8 oz) of marzipan to make the fruit. Roll out the remaining marzipan so that it is large enough to cover the top and sides of each cake. Cover and smooth the cakes as shown on pages 8–9. Set aside to dry for about 12 hours.

1

Carved out cake

3 Roll out the remaining white sugar paste, brush the marzipan with cooled boiled water and cover the top and sides of both cakes with the sugar paste, using the method on page 9. Trim off the excess. Leave to dry for about 2 hours then place the bottom cake in the centre of the covered drum board. Dowel the bottom tier as shown on page 10. Place the top tier centrally onto the bottom tier using a little royal icing to stick the tiers together. With white royal icing and the No. 5 piping nozzle, pipe a shell border around the base of each tier to hide the join.

4 Use the marzipan set aside from Step 2 to make the fruit.

To make the apples
This quantity makes six apples
◆ 300 g (10½ oz) green-coloured marzipan

Divide the green marzipan into six equal portions and roll each into a ball, smoothing out any cracks with the palms of your hands. Mark the top and bottom with the star tool and leave to dry. Using a small amount of brown marzipan, make six stalks and secure them to the top of each apple

with sugar glue. Dust with red dust to give a blush and leave to harden.

To make the oranges
This quantity makes six oranges
◆ 300 g (10½ oz) orange-coloured marzipan

Divide the marzipan into six equal portions and roll each into a ball, smoothing out any cracks with the palms of your hands. Gently roll each ball over a grater to mark the skin. Mark the top and bottom with the star tool and leave to harden.

To make the pears

This quantity makes four pears

◆ 240 g (8½ oz) green-coloured marzipan

◆ Small amount of brown marzipan

Divide the green marzipan into four equal portions and roll each into a ball, smoothing out any cracks with the palms of your hands. Shape each ball into a pear shape and mark the top and bottom with the star tool. Using a small amount of brown marzipan, make four stalks and secure them to the top of each pear with sugar glue. Dust with red dust to give a blush and leave to harden.

To make the strawberries

This quantity makes 16 strawberries

◆ 240 g (8½ oz) red-coloured marzipan

◆ Small amount of green marzipan

Divide the red marzipan into 16 equal portions and roll each into a ball, smoothing out any cracks with the palms of your hands. Shape each ball into a strawberry shape and gently roll over a grater to mark the skin. Using the calyx cutter, cut out 16 calyxes in green marzipan and place one on top

of each strawberry sticking them down with a little sugar glue. Leave to harden.

To make the cherries

This quantity makes eight cherries

◆ 80 g (3 oz) red-coloured marzipan

◆ Small amount of green marzipan

Divide the red marzipan into 8 equal portions and roll each into a ball, smoothing out any cracks with the palms of your hands. Mark the top with the ball tool. Using a small amount of green marzipan, make eight stalks and stick them into the top of each cherry with sugar glue. Leave to harden.

To make the bananas

This quantity makes four bananas

◆ 240 g (8½ oz) yellow-coloured marzipan

Divide the marzipan into 4 equal portions and roll each into a ball then into a sausage shape thinner at either end, smoothing out any cracks with the palms of your hands. Flatten the sides of the sausage shape and give the banana a slight bend. Paint fine lines with brown food colouring as seen in picture and leave to harden.

To make the pineapple

This quantity makes one pineapple

◆ 350 g (12½ oz) orange-coloured marzipan

◆ 50 g (2 oz) green flower paste

Roll the marzipan into a ball then into a flat oval shape, smoothing out any cracks with the palms of your hands. Mark as shown (*see pic 3*), pinching the marzipan between your fingers to achieve the desired effect. Cut out leaf shapes out of the flower paste and, when hardened, stick them into the top of the pineapple with sugar glue. Dab the tips of the pineapple with brown food colouring and leave to harden.

3

Moulding the pineapple

To make the lemons

This quantity makes five lemons

◆ 250 g (9 oz) yellow-coloured marzipan

Divide the marzipan into 5 equal portions and roll each into a ball, smoothing out any cracks with the palms of your hands. Shape each ball into an oval shape, extending the ends into points and gently roll over a grater to mark the skin. Leave to harden.

To make the plums

This quantity makes 10 plums

◆ 150 g (5½ oz) plum-coloured marzipan

Divide the marzipan into 10 equal

2

Making the fruit shapes

portions. Roll each piece into a ball then into an oval shape. Using a cocktail stick, mark a line down the centre. Leave to harden.

To make the grapes
This quantity makes 36 grapes
◆ 180 g (6½ oz) green-coloured marzipan
◆ 180 g (6½ oz) purple-coloured marzipan

Divide each colour of marzipan into 18 equal portions. Roll each piece into a ball then into an oval shape. Stick the grapes to each other with dabs of sugar glue to form bunches when placing them on the cake.

To make the berries
This quantity makes enough to fill any gaps
◆ 50 g (2 oz) blue-coloured marzipan
◆ 50 g (2 oz) red-coloured marzipan

Roll the marzipan into small balls in both colours. Use to fill in any gaps between the fruits and stick in place with sugar glue.

5 Stick the fruits to the cake with royal icing, stacking them from the bottom upwards, keeping an even look to the fruits (*see pic 4*). Finally, decorate the edge of the drum board with white ribbon.

Positioning the fruit

Suppliers

UNITED KINGDOM
Cel Crafts
Springfield House
Gate Helmsley
York YO41 1NF
Tel: +44 (0)1759 371447
Fax: +44 (0)1759 372513

Culpitt Ltd
Jubilee Industrial Estate
Ashington
Northumberland NE63 8UQ
Tel: +44 (0)1670 814545
Fax : +44 (0)1670 815248
Web: www.culpitt.com

The Elite Cake Company
5 Havelock Street
Blyth
Northumberland NE24 1AB
Tel: +44 (0)1670 365241

Patchwork Cutters
3 Raines Close
Greasby
Wirral

Merseyside CH49 2BB
Tel: +44 (0)151 678 5053

NORTH AMERICA
Creative Tools Ltd
3 Tannery Court
Richmond Hill
Ontario
Canada L4C 7V5

Home Cake Artistry Inc.
1002 North Central
Suite 511
Richardson
Texas 75080
USA

Wilton Enterprises Inc.
2240 West 75th Street
Woodridge
Illinois 60517
USA
Tel: +1 630 963 1818
Fax: +1 630 963 7196
Web: www.wilton.com

Wilton Industries Canada
98 Carrier Drive
Etobicoke
Ontario
Canada M9W5R1
Tel: +1 416 679 0790
Fax: +1 416 679-0798

AUSTRALIA & NEW ZEALAND
Fer Lewis, Cake Ornament Co.
156 Alfred Street
Fortitude Valley
Brisbane 4006
Australia

Decor Cakes
Shop 12
Victoria Arcade
Otahuhu
Auckland
New Zealand
Tel: +64 (0)9 276 6676
Web: www.decorcakes.co.nz

Templates

All templates are 100% actual size.

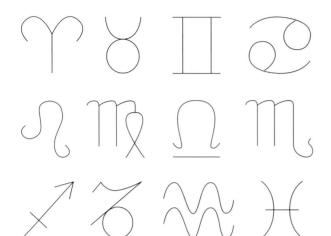

Out of this world, page 34

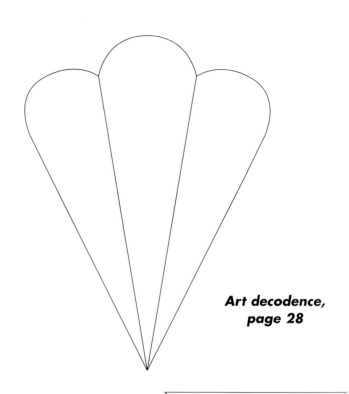

Art decodence, page 28

Babe in the woods, page 22

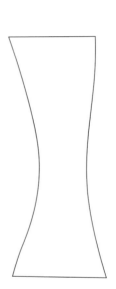

Masquerade, page 44

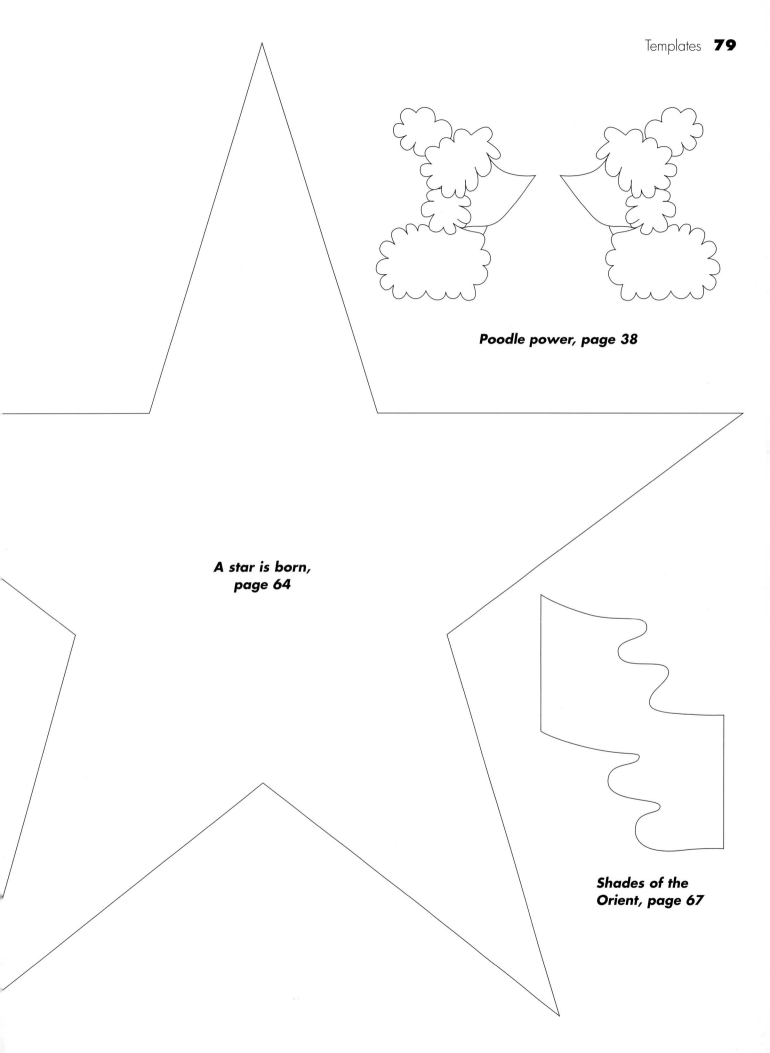

Poodle power, page 38

*A star is born,
page 64*

*Shades of the
Orient, page 67*

Index